LIFE LESSONS FROM OVER THE RAINBOW

Emeralds
of Oz

Peter Guzzardi

HARPER WAVE

An Imprint of HarperCollins*Publishers*

HarperCollins books may be purchased for educational, business, or sales promotional use. For information, please email the Special Markets Department at SPsales@harpercollins.com.

FIRST EDITION

DESIGNED BY BONNI LEON-BERMAN

Library of Congress Cataloging-in-Publication Data has been applied for.

ISBN 978-0-06-234877-7

19 20 21 22 23 LSC 10 9 8 7 6 5 4 3 2 1

To the Young in Heart

There is no path to truth.

Truth must be discovered

But there is no formula for its discovery.

You must set out on the uncharted sea

And the uncharted sea is your self.

–KRISHNAMURTI

Contents

Emeralds of Oz

PART ONE

Following the Yellow Brick Road

ONE DAY WHILE I was visiting a friend in New York, a book on his shelf caught my eye. Oversized and dramatic, its jacket featured an image of Judy Garland in the blue-and-white gingham frock she wore as Dorothy in *The Wizard of Oz*. As I leafed through its pages, I was struck by a thought. During my long career as a book editor, I've brushed up against a lot of wisdom, yet so much of what I learned was right there in this extraordinary film I first watched as a child. As luck would have it, I mentioned this insight aloud to that friend, who happened to be a publisher with whom I'd worked on various books as a freelance editor. He responded to my idea with unexpected enthusiasm and suggested I write it up as a book proposal.

Five years later I finished writing this book, and during that time it has become something I never expected: timely. When authoritarian leaders are springing up around the world, *The Wizard of Oz* invites us not to be distracted by their misleading sounds and optics, but to pull back the curtain on the truth. When consumerism keeps tugging us into an endless pursuit of more, it's life-changing to consider that we already possess what we long for most. When fear seems to be gaining the upper hand, it's reassuring to watch it shrivel at the cleansing touch of water. And when I consider how much Glinda's ultimate words of wisdom mean to me ("You've always had the power to go back to Kansas"), I realize they led me to fulfill a lifelong desire by writing a book that captures the life-affirming wisdom of Oz.

I also discovered a magical self-help tool embodied in the film, but more on this later.

I was eleven years old when the wisdom of Oz first entered my life. My family joined millions of others in what was only just becoming an annual American tradition. We gathered around the television in our suburban home to watch a film in which a cyclone lifts young Dorothy Gale out of Kansas and transports her to the Land of Oz. Color TV was still an expensive novelty in 1961, so my parents, siblings, and I sat around our black-and-white RCA Victor to watch the CBS special presentation.

Even without the impact of the film's dramatic Technicolor, I'll never forget Dorothy stepping from her airlifted farmhouse into the glistening miracle of Munchkinland. Or my terror at the cackling malevolence of the Wicked Witch of the West, the booming voice of the Wizard of Oz, and the soaring menace of the Winged Monkeys. Or the relief I felt when Dorothy made it safely home to Kansas in the end. Looking back on it now, I see that the film struck just the right balance between terror and reassurance. MGM's masterpiece was scary enough to sear itself into the viewer's psyche, yet it was also buoyed by enough slapstick humor, song and dance, and acts of kindness to reassure us that, like Dorothy, you and I can successfully navigate the path to our own heart's desire.

A Cyclone Lifts the House

When I was a toddler, I nearly died. At the time, my family was living in Djakarta, Indonesia, where my father worked for the State Department. It was the early 1950s, and polio was on a global rampage. Some of the millions of cases were mild enough to be mistaken for flu, but others were deadly. Mine was on the serious side. Isolated by doctors fearing contagion, I lay in a hospital crib as the virus moved through my body, leaving paralysis in its wake. Just before reaching my respiratory system, however, it stopped. I was lucky—no iron lung, no lifetime in a wheelchair—although when the disease receded its effects lingered in my feet and legs. In my earliest memories I'm being strapped into braces before bedtime. Eventually I would learn to walk, then run, but I always moved with less ease than other children.

My limited mobility stayed with me through the rituals of boyhood and growing up. When other kids played basketball and baseball, I struggled to keep pace. When teams were chosen during gym class, I was always among the last to be picked. To escape indignities like these, which loom so large in the life of a child, I sought refuge in movies and books. In novels, especially, I found magical access to qualities I longed to possess.

Immersed in weekly finds from the local library, I became as resourceful as the Hardy boys, as morally upright as Zane Grey's riders of the purple sage, as courageous as Edgar Rice Burroughs's Tarzan and John Carter of Mars, as patrician as Mary Renault's rulers of ancient Greece, and as gallant as Sir Galahad in his pursuit of the Holy Grail. Books rescued me from the heartache of childhood loneliness and freed me from the limitations of my body as if by a wave of Merlin's—or Glinda's—wand. Books took me over the rainbow.

The Scarecrow, Tin Man, and Cowardly Lion All in One

Over the rainbow I might have stayed, wandering through fantastical literary worlds, had I not met John Coster. After my family left Indonesia for Rome, Italy, where my father worked at Time Life for nearly a decade, we moved back to the U.S. and the house where my mother was born—in Bronxville, a suburb of New York City known for its affluence and conservatism. At the time, the public school included just one black child and one Jewish child. Martin Luther King Jr. picked Bronxville for a march down Main Street on behalf of black workers in the local hospital. Into this bastion of homogeneity came I, a gangly, bespectacled child from Italy, followed a year later by John Coster, a six-foot-five-inch sixth grader transplanted from Havana, Cuba. Americans? Yes. Accepted? Not so much—at least that's how it felt to us.

Thrown together by fate, John and I became fast friends. After school we'd play Risk or Stratego at my house, or go over to John's and listen to rock 'n' roll records belonging to his older siblings. One afternoon during that first snowy winter of our friendship, John's father drove us to the town of Tuckahoe, site of a huge hill known for superb sledding. John and I enjoyed ourselves all afternoon until dusk descended. Our pants and gloves were sodden and the temperature was dropping fast, yet there was no sign of John's dad, who had promised to return in a few hours.

John and I waited awhile longer as the last stragglers headed home, until finally there was nothing left to do but begin the long trek back. We stayed with the main road at first, dragging our sleds through the freezing slush, but when it became clear that John's dad wasn't coming, we began taking shortcuts through neighboring side streets. Now it was *really* getting cold. Not the hardiest physical specimen, I began to worry about whether I was going to survive.

Then I remembered something. I had a box of chocolates in my knapsack, a Whitman's Sampler I had bought for my father, whose birthday was coming up. Awkwardly tearing off the cellophane with numb fingers I shared small, life-giving bites of chocolate with John during that endless, bone-chilling slog, nursing our supply until we finally made it all the way back to his house.

John's father was profusely apologetic for forgetting to pick us up. As John and I thawed out and regaled his brother and sisters with the tale of our heroic journey, I knew the two of us had passed an important milestone together. It would be the first of many in a lifetime as best friends, making our way through our own version of hostile woods, Deadly Poppy Fields, and unreliable authority figures.

It wasn't until many years later that I realized I was about the same age as Dorothy when John and I nearly froze on the way home from sledding. Looking back on my life, I can see dozens of parallels with Dorothy's journey. Just as her frightening experience with Miss Gulch in Kansas forced Dorothy to make her own way, my lesson in survival gave me the first inkling that I could take care of myself. Her longing for a place that was trouble free sent her over the rainbow, much like my longing to transcend the limits of my body launched me into the world of books. Her desire for friends—and compassion for their plight—connected her to the Scarecrow, Tin Man, and Cowardly Lion, who served much the same role in her life as John Coster did in mine. In yet another parallel, Dorothy's final hard-won discovery in the film did not come easily in my life, either. . . .

There's No Place Like Home

My wife had planned a monthlong family road trip out west. The ambitious itinerary included camping and hiking at famous national parks: Arches, the Grand Tetons, Glacier, and Yellowstone. Some sites were remote, but our two sons were fit from running cross-country and playing Ultimate Frisbee, and my wife loves strenuous exercise. Physically, I was the weak link.

Our first destination was the Maroon Bells in Colorado. There in the White River National Forest a tumbling waterfall feeds a pristine mountain lake nestled between two fourteen-thousand-foot peaks, its remote beauty protected by a limited number of campsites. We had gotten a late start to our day, so it was mid-afternoon before we got to the parking lot where we'd begin to hike in. To reach the campsite before dark we had to move quickly, so my wife, Isabel, and our older son, Sam, set off, leaving my younger son, William, and me to follow at my slower pace.

I pulled on my backpack but didn't walk more than a few hundred yards before realizing I might be in trouble. At an altitude of nearly ten thousand feet the oxygen was much thinner than I was used to, and I hadn't hiked with a full backpack in decades. Half an hour later I was fighting panic. Try as I might I couldn't take in a satisfying lungful of air. William came to my aid. "Dad, I'll carry your backpack. You just walk for fifty steps and then stop to catch your breath. When you're ready we'll take the next fifty steps."

My son's reassuring strategy worked, and as darkness closed in we used our flashlights to navigate the remaining distance to the lake, where the tents had been set up. I was relieved to be reunited with Sam and Isabel, but the fuse of my anxiety had been lit and it wasn't going out. I lay in my sleeping bag too worried about my effortful breathing to sleep. Every few hours I made my way down to the mountain lake and splashed frigid water on my face, but even that only momentarily distracted me from my fears.

Somehow, I made it through the night, but as we continued our road trip I imagined more and more reasons to feel panicky, including thin air, grizzly bear attacks, mudslides, and earthquakes. One morning, while sitting in the back seat of the car riding through the Grand Tetons, I reached my breaking point: the pain of living with my fears had become unbearable. I decided to let my mind die—to let go of the inner voice that I identified as me. This was terrifying in itself, but by now I felt I had nothing to lose.

It took several tries, but finally my mind melted like the Wicked Witch of the West under Dorothy's bucket of water. Immediately I felt this extraordinary sensation. Looking out the car window *I was* the trees, the mountain grasses, the craggy rocks overlooking the road, the vast sky overhead, and the tarmac unspooling before us as we drove. By letting go of my thoughts, I slipped into a state of pure awareness. By severing the connection to my individual self, I merged into the oneness within us all. I had traveled beyond fear, or the need for safety. I had clicked my heels three times and returned home.

Since then I've learned that this experience of unity consciousness is often induced by unbearable life circumstances, as reported by Eckhart Tolle and Byron Katie, among many others who have experienced it. My immersion lasted only an hour or so, but that mystical experience of being home ripples through my life to this day.

My Many Glindas

When it came time to choose a profession, the child who spent endless nights in bed reading under the covers with a flashlight became an adult who earned his livelihood working with books and authors. Over more than four decades in book publishing, I've enjoyed the great good fortune to edit a remarkable constellation of writers. This diverse group ranges from astrophysicist Stephen Hawking to novelist Douglas Adams, from Carol Burnett to Deepak Chopra, from Queen Noor to M. Scott Peck, from Geneen Roth to Kareem Abdul-Jabbar, from Arianna Huffington to Bobby Kennedy Jr., from Susan Cain to Martin Amis. As my colleague Ian Ballantine, founder of the first American paperback publishing house, once told me, "Book publishing offers us the opportunity to associate with the finest minds of our time." I couldn't agree more, and I've tried to make the most of it.

Along the way, the insights that I've gleaned from years of working with these brilliant people have felt oddly familiar. It took half a century after first watching *The Wizard of Oz* before I had that epiphany about just how much life-enhancing acumen was already embodied in that classic American fairy tale. Much like Dorothy with her Ruby Slippers, I had to go on a quest to experience life for myself—as well as vicariously through my authors—before I could appreciate what was in my possession all along.

While editing Stephen Hawking's *A Brief History of Time*, I learned about the quest for the Holy Grail of astrophysics, a Grand Unified Theory that could marry the two greatest—but still separate—theoretical breakthroughs of our time: quantum mechanics and general relativity. If we ever make this discovery we will have truly pulled back the curtain, for, as Stephen put it, "then we would know the mind of God." While working with Deepak Chopra on dozens of books, I learned about the ancient Vedic wisdom of India, and its assertion that there is no "out there" at all. Nothing exists until we summon it into being through our individual awareness; before that moment, it's all cosmic soup, a sea of pure potential that is home to everything in the universe.

Working with Byron Katie and Stephen Mitchell, I learned about seeing things as if for the first time, the key to Dorothy's success in Oz. Geneen Roth showed me how addiction can be addressed by turning to powers beyond the physical realm, much like the Scarecrow and Tin Man did in the Deadly Poppy Field. Douglas Adams, Carol Burnett, and Paula Poundstone taught me that laughter (think Cowardly Lion) creates a kinship like no other, especially when it's not at someone else's expense. Larry Dossey helped me see my experience in the Grand Tetons in the context of what he calls One Mind. Debbie Ford made me aware that emotions we suppress, like anger, have a silver lining that Dorothy puts to good use. Cheryl Richardson deepened my appreciation for being vulnerable like the Tin Man, with his big heart. From each of hundreds of authors, I've learned something useful that more often than not echoes wisdom in *The Wizard of Oz*.

Why *The Wizard of Oz*?

Lots of movies offer valuable life lessons, yet this one stands head and shoulders above the rest. Today, eight decades after its Hollywood premiere on August 15, 1939, it's still remarkably alive in our cultural consciousness—you need only look to contemporary hits like *The Wiz* or *Wicked* to see its influence. The film is also mentioned time and again in songs, movies, TV shows, books, articles, blog posts, cartoons, podcasts, and conversations. What makes it so special? Why is this the most watched film of all time?

Stories become classics when they tune in to fundamental aspects of our shared human experience.

We can all relate to Beowulf's courage in confronting a man-eating monster, to Ulysses's ten-year struggle to return home to his wife and family, and to Romeo and Juliet's defiance of a deadly feud between their families. We root for Frodo in his selfless quest to end Sauron's threat to Middle Earth, and for young Harry Potter in his unlikely challenge to the vast, nihilistic powers of Voldemort. Dark forces have been unleashed in the world. We may feel helpless against them, yet evil must be vanquished and goodness renewed. We must fight the tendency to sleepwalk through our lives, and awaken. This is the fundamental aspect of the Hero's Journey.

At first, Dorothy Gale seems an unlikely hero. In Kansas, the twelve-year-old is no match for a vengeful neighbor determined to destroy Dorothy's beloved dog. However, by the film's end she has prevailed over two wicked witches and a notorious wizard, helped her friends achieve their heart's desire, and finally attained her own. She starts off as a child, but by the final scene she's every bit the equal of the adults gathering around her recovery bed. During the course of her journey, viewers arrive at insights that are the hallmark of every classic book or film. Gems of wisdom, large and small, have been embedded in the path to the Emerald City to ensure that we are not just entertained and inspired, but also enlightened.

There's no doubt that much of the magic of the MGM film based on L. Frank Baum's book *The Wonderful Wizard of Oz* emanates from masterly screenwriting, directing, original music, acting, lighting, big-budget sets, and special effects. Yet that enchantment would have dimmed over the years without the seeds of wisdom the film plants in our psyches as children, when we're most receptive. Once set in the loamy soil of our imagination, these insights germinate and then blossom like moonflowers over the course of a lifetime, as conditions become favorable. This is perennially true for viewers of *The Wizard of Oz*, generation after generation.

One of the marvels of this film is that it resonates with so many different people in so many different ways. Psychologists see in it evidence of the theories of Freud, Jung, and D. W. Winnicott. Philosophers identify the ideas of Plato, Socrates, and Kant at work. One economist famously viewed *The Wizard of Oz* as a coded treatise on the gold standard. Historians see evidence of L. Frank Baum's belief in Theosophy, a religious movement based on the direct experience of divinity.

The Wizard of Oz is a kaleidoscope. Each viewer gives it a distinctive twist and is rewarded with an individual mosaic of insights. In this particular book I'm reporting on what I see through the peephole of my own life experience—some of which I've shared here. But I have no special claim to the wisdom of Oz. In fact, like the preacher who gives the sermons he needs to hear, I'm very much still learning these lessons myself. However, with any luck my observations will complement your own, or prompt new ones, as you read the pages ahead. And perhaps our Yellow Brick Roads will converge in a wood—or a bookstore—where we can meet and discuss what you've discovered.

Now a brief word of warning to fellow seekers about spelunking for wisdom in the caverns of Oz. For all the wealth of insights in this film, they're not always easily found. A few gems are lying on the ground in plain sight, like "there's no place like home," but after that the mission becomes more challenging. There's a historical reason for this. In writing *The Wonderful Wizard of Oz*, L. Frank Baum (the *L* stands for *Lyman*, a name he did not like) made a conscious decision to break with the past and forge a new creative direction.

At the time Baum was writing, at the tail end of the nineteenth century, fairy tales had long been the province of Germany's brothers Grimm. They were written to provide moral lessons reinforced by terrifying witches, wicked stepmothers, and cannibalistic old ladies living in the woods. However, Baum believed those moral principles were now being sufficiently taught in school, freeing him up to write a new kind of modern fairy tale emphasizing wonder and joy. Although years later MGM Studios would add a megadose of the scariness that Baum had taken such pains to avoid, the film does take its cues from him when it comes to morality. The lessons of Oz are largely hidden from view, where they won't distract from the film's ability to entertain.

How to Read This Book

Before we continue, an important bit of topography. In the next section you'll find numbered insights arranged in the order I found them, along the arc of Dorothy's journey of discovery in the film. My fondest hope is that one or more of these might trigger in you a spontaneous shift in awareness, like a new pair of glasses with the right correction for astigmatism. Suddenly your familiar world may look brighter, crisper, and generally cheerier.

Along with smaller—and sometimes lighthearted—

insights, you will also come across nine large gems that I've identified as Emeralds of Wisdom. They form the heart of this book. You'll find these Emeralds interspersed throughout the other insights but numbered separately. Later I will invite you to view the nine Emeralds of Wisdom again, this time as part of a larger whole. Seen this way they become a powerful tool that can be applied to any obstacle, large or small. Reviewing these Emeralds activates their magical inner powers just the way Dorothy did, easing your way on your own Hero's Journey.

Lastly, in the appendix you'll find a brief history of the book and the film, along with some tidbits about the making of the film itself.

Now, however, it's time to sit back and savor the pages that lie ahead, allowing the many joys and insights of *The Wizard of Oz* to wash over you, mingling with and enriching your own.

PART TWO

The Wisdom of Oz

IN KANSAS

On rereading L. Frank Baum's *The Wonderful Wizard of Oz* as an adult, I was surprised by how little time we spend in Kansas. No time at all, really. In the first few pages we're introduced to Aunt Em and Uncle Henry, and given a brief description of the one-room farmhouse they share with their niece, Dorothy. Baum quickly sketches the sunbaked Kansas landscape and its weather-beaten inhabitants in shades of gray, with the exception of Toto and Dorothy. No sooner is this stage set than the wind picks up, and Uncle Henry recognizes the signs. A cyclone is coming, and within moments it lifts up Dorothy, Toto, and the family farmhouse and carries us all off to Oz.

In Baum's book, Oz is a real place, isolated from the rest of the world by vast deserts and towering mountain ranges. Oz's exotic inhabitants, however, are unlike anything we've ever seen before. They include beasts with bodies like bears and heads like tigers, fragile people made of china, and fierce folk who launch their hammer-heads from spring-loaded necks to knock down trespassers. These fantastical elements of the story, originally illustrated by W. W. Denslow, helped Frank Baum's children's book become a best seller. However, some forty years later MGM viewed them as an obstacle to a successful film.

The studio was concerned that if its story followed Baum's original too closely, the film would be pigeon-holed as fantasy, a tough sell to moviegoers in the late 1930s for anyone but Walt Disney. In order to make Oz less fanciful, MGM added the trusty trope of The Dream. This required expanding events in Kansas by creating new scenes and characters that would later echo in Dorothy's subconscious. The film's scriptwriters added farmhands Hunk, Hickory, and Zeke, who would reappear in Oz as the Scarecrow,

Tin Man, and the Cowardly Lion, respectively; Miss Almira Gulch, who would become the Wicked Witch of the West; and Professor Marvel, who would play multiple roles in Oz, including gatekeeper to Emerald City, driver of the hansom cab, palace guard, and the Wizard of Oz himself. New scenes populated by these characters included Miss Gulch's visit, Toto's escape from her bicycle basket, Dorothy's runaway encounter with Professor Marvel, and her desperate dash home just as the cyclone hits.

Introducing The Dream to the creative mix may not have been the most original solution to MGM's problem, but it paid off in ways its creators may not have anticipated. It allowed the story to plumb hidden depths, first in the subconscious mind with all its rich layers of meaning and symbolism, and then in the Jungian realm of the collective unconscious, the wellspring of archetypes and myths. Mother, father, trickster, crone, unexpected allies, a harrowing trial, and a great reward: these are the elements of a Hero's Journey, and now of a film fairy tale that would pass the greatest trial of all—the test of time.

MGM'S ICONIC LION EMITS a thunderous roar. Clouds drift behind the film's titles and the dedication to "the

Young in Heart." Then a twelve-year-old girl is running down a rutted dirt road, clutching her schoolbooks to her chest and looking back apprehensively. She's upset, something to do with the dog trotting alongside her. *"She isn't coming yet, Toto. Did she hurt you? No, but she tried to, didn't she?"* Finally reaching the farmhouse where she lives, Dorothy pushes open the gate, eager to tell her aunt and uncle what happened on her way home from school. We're approaching the film's first insight.

1. There are no mistakes, only lessons.

One message I absorbed in school as a child was the importance of not making a mistake. I observed that there are right answers and wrong answers for every question, and success depends on sorting one from the other. Fortunately, this misguided binary approach to learning eventually gave way to curiosity, but I might have been spared that delay if I had been aware of this first insight from Oz: there are no mistakes, only lessons.

As the film begins, Dorothy finds herself in a dilemma. Her beloved terrier enjoys chasing a cat that belongs to the notoriously unpleasant Almira Gulch. Hunk, the farmhand who becomes the Scarecrow, does his best to get Dorothy to use her brains to resolve the problem. "When you come home, don't go by Miss Gulch's place. Then Toto won't get in her garden, and you won't get in no trouble, see?"

Imagine for a moment a parallel universe in which Dorothy takes Hunk's advice. No Toto chasing Miss Gulch's cat. No Miss Gulch carting Toto off to his doom, prompting Dorothy and Toto to run away once the little dog makes his escape. No being locked outside the storm cellar when the cyclone hits. No flying window frame knocking Dorothy unconscious, triggering "Dorothy's delirium," as the film's creators called her dream, therefore no journey through Oz. It's anybody's guess where that story might have taken us, but it's safe to say that it would not have led to the most-watched film of all time. Instead of reading these words, you might be reading a book about a runner-up, like *Wisdom from* The Godfather: *Life Lessons You Can't Refuse.*

The point is this: although ignoring Hunk's advice may seem like an error in judgment, Dorothy made no mistake by allowing Toto to chase Miss Gulch's cat. There was no right or wrong decision. That's not a useful distinction to make when it comes to learning, or life. Instead we make choices, and we learn from them. That's what Dorothy did, and she reaped the results; had she not done so, both she and we would have been much the poorer for it.

2. When it's important to speak your mind, keep at it.

Try as Dorothy might—and she does try mightily— once she gets back to the farm after school, Dorothy can't get anyone to pay attention. Aunt Em and Uncle Henry are busy counting chicks in a broken-down incubator, and their three farmhands are caught up in repairing an old wagon and feeding pigs. Dorothy gets points for persistence, though, and it's this tenacity in speaking her mind that offers up the insight here. She is not going to be silenced, even in the face of steady rejection and some teasing.

When social scientists conduct research to identify those qualities that separate top performers from the rest, one stands out: good old-fashioned grit. When harnessed to speaking up, this quality can make all the difference—whether you're communicating needs to your spouse, contributing ideas to that crucial meeting at work, or advocating for someone who could use a helping hand. In the larger world, grit in service of suppressed voices provides a potent catalyst for social change. In Dorothy's case, not only has her tenacity earned our admiration, but her frustration prompts her to sing "Somewhere Over the Rainbow." This, as we'll see soon in the first Emerald of Wisdom, changes everything.

3. When a child keeps trying to tell you something, stop and listen (no matter how busy you are).

Not only is this an act of kindness, but it may also save you embarrassment, or even bigger trouble. That child may be trying to point out spinach on your front tooth, or that you've left your pocketbook on the front hall table, or that your house is on fire. In Aunt Em and Uncle Henry's case, if either of them had listened to the story Dorothy was so eager to tell, they wouldn't have been blindsided by Miss Gulch's furious onslaught. With a bit of warning, they might have avoided giving up Toto, having their niece run away, and the near-tragic events that followed.

EMERALD OF WISDOM

1

Listen to your longing.

At the beginning of *The Wizard of Oz*, there's little to indicate that we're watching one of the greatest films ever made. A schoolgirl runs home eager to share something that just happened, but everyone's too busy to listen. So far, nothing out of the ordinary. Then, suddenly, everything changes. Dorothy steps into the barnyard, and as she begins to sing the sun-bleached world vanishes. Like a genie summoned from Aladdin's lamp, Dorothy's voice sweeps us up on a magic carpet ride of longing so deep and so wide that everything else disappears from view. This one song changes everything, swooping and soaring, achingly sad yet buoyant with hope.

What does Dorothy long for? She tells us it's

a faraway place where troubles melt like lemon drops, but such places are difficult even to imagine. Certainly Oz, the land Dorothy imagines in her upcoming dream, will fall far short of trouble free, with its wicked witches, fraudulent wizard, and fierce Winged Monkeys. To meet its challenges, Dorothy will need to draw on all her inner resources. So, what is Dorothy *really* longing for?

By the end of the film, we will possess new insight into the ultimate source of her yearning, but now, at the outset of the story, Dorothy longs more than anything *to belong*. In social primates this need is based on survival: if you're not accepted, you're left behind. Perennially underfoot, Dorothy yearns to be included, to be heard and recognized. In the film the absence of Dorothy's parents goes unexplained, but from Frank Baum's book we learn that Dorothy is an orphan. No details are given, but none are needed: the most natural source of affection for a child has been denied her. This is the ultimate unrequited love, and Dorothy's longing to span that unbridgeable gulf evokes one of the great love songs of all time.

This feeling contributes to the urgency that makes "Over the Rainbow" so unforgettable—and so universal. Who hasn't felt unwanted? Who hasn't yearned to belong? Who hasn't lost their parents, if only for a little while? Viewers of the film who may have been ambivalent until this moment are completely hooked by the time Dorothy finishes her song and leans her head on Toto. Now it's clear that this is no ordinary movie: we're about to embark on a mythic, transcendent journey fueled by the fathomless depths of a young girl's longing.

Yearning arises when the gulf between what you desire and what you possess becomes too great, which makes it all-important to recognize this feeling when it shows up in your life. It's putting you on notice. When it gets strong enough it will cast you off from your safe mooring and send you swirling into the unknown. Longing is a herald announcing that change is on the way, hurtling toward you like a cyclone across a Kansas prairie.

4. When change comes knocking, answer the door.

Sometimes the signs are obvious: a relationship breaks up; a company offers you a new job; an opportunity arises to take a trip, or start a business. Sometimes the indications are subtler: activities that used to bring you pleasure have lost their charge. Either way, an invitation to try something new will follow that surge of longing as surely as day follows night. So keep an eye out for it, and step up to the occasion when it arises.

Of course, there is an alternative. Scholar and author Joseph Campbell, ebullient cohost of the popular PBS television documentary *The Power of Myth*, calls this response to the Hero's Journey "refusal of the call." There's no shame in it. We've all been there. But there is a price to be paid. When you consistently choose the familiar over the unknown, you're walling yourself in. You're turning your back on the great, endless cycle of sacrifice and renewal to cling to the vain hope that your present life can remain just the way it is. Trapped by the ego's childish desires, you're declining individuation and with it the rich experiences of adulthood. Sound good? No, not to me, either.

Even when we choose to, we can't always turn away from the call to embark on a spiritual quest. We can hide from the messenger, but there will come a time when those papers get served. A twister will come along and airlift us over the rainbow, like it or not. Better to push past the fear and answer the call on your own terms. Perform a song at open mic night. Adopt a pet. Hike the Andes. Volunteer at a soup kitchen. Start a business that makes a difference. Once you recognize that change is knocking, open the door.

5. When you feel a song welling up inside you, belt it out.

There's a reason why people sing the blues when times are hard: somehow, inexplicably, the burden feels lighter. Whether I'm harmonizing in choir or accompanying myself with a few simple chords on guitar, singing brings me joy like few things in life. If you struggle to stay on key, no worries. Judy Garland was one of a kind. If the shower is the venue you're most comfortable with, that's great, but all of us have songs to sing. When the spirit moves you, sing it loud and sing it proud. There's magic at work. Give it every chance to make its way out into the world, where we need all the enchantment we can get.

6. Beware of sticklers for the law— especially when it benefits them.

With just a smidgen of forethought Dorothy could have avoided infuriating a powerful neighbor. So why didn't she? Well, it's one way for a child to get adult attention. And in this case it works. When Miss Gulch comes riding over to the Gale family farm on her sensible, black Ladies Safety Model 1900 Orient bicycle, all hell breaks loose.

Miss Gulch claims Toto bit her, and that "there's a law protecting folks against dogs that bite!" If Aunt Em and Uncle Henry don't go along, she'll bring down a lawsuit that could result in the loss of their farm. Dorothy's caregivers are quick to capitulate, which is understandable given that Miss Gulch owns half the county. But it's not advisable, which leads us to these next few insights from Oz.

When the law becomes a tool for justifying something you know in your heart is wrong (could Toto really pose a threat to Almira Gulch?), push back. Miss Gulch has a "zero tolerance" policy for kids and dogs. Keep a weather eye out for this term. It's a sign that a person or group is being singled out for falling short of perfection. The next thing you know, that person could be you. Zero tolerance is just another way of saying compassion-free.

7. Read the fine print.

I know, I know. Who has time? But much like listening to a persistent child, this insight from Oz ends up saving both time and trouble. When Miss Gulch hands Aunt Em a piece of paper, ostensibly a sheriff's order giving Miss Gulch the right to take Toto, Dorothy's aunt passes it directly to Uncle Henry. He gives it only a cursory glance before the two of them cave in to Miss Gulch's demands.

Hold it right there! Freeze the frame! Someone in that room should be taking a moment to read the document carefully. Miss Gulch claims it gives her the right to take Toto away in her basket, but why take her word for it? Her story keeps changing. At one point she claims it will be up to the sheriff to decide if Toto should be tied up, but moments later she states that she's going to make sure he's destroyed. What does that document actually *say*?

Depending on whom you ask, either God or the devil is in the details. So take a closer look. You may as well know which one you're dealing with.

8. Don't say yes the first time you're asked for something you don't want to give up.

We've established that Aunt Em and Uncle Henry should read that document from the sheriff more carefully, yet this is just part of a larger issue. Dorothy's caregivers need to do a better job of standing up for Dorothy and Toto. What could they do differently? They could ask for more time to consider the problem. Suggest a meeting with the sheriff to seek a reasonable solution to the dispute. Tell Almira Gulch that they'd like to call a cousin in Omaha who went to law school and read him the sheriff's letter over the phone. Sometimes it's just not a good idea to be accommodating—at least not right off the bat.

Dorothy understands this. She doesn't back down from Miss Gulch. Aunt Em and Uncle Henry, on the other hand, err on the side of being too nice. Uncle Henry is good-natured but conflict avoidant. Aunt Em is hemmed in by her own sense of the right way to behave, which leads us directly to . . .

9. Don't let virtue keep you from speaking your mind.

I feel bad for Aunt Em when she tells Almira Gulch, "I've been dying to tell you what I thought of you . . . and now . . . well—being a Christian woman—I can't say it!" The poor woman is clearly frustrated by her sense of duty, if not to be kind then at least not to be *unkind*. But instead of allowing this obligation to stifle her, Aunt Em could find a way to speak her mind without being rude or hurtful.

My mother, who learned her manners in the South, placed a high value on politeness. It certainly makes social interactions more pleasant, and Dorothy's good manners will serve her well on the Yellow Brick Road, as we'll see. Yet there are times when being polite contributes unnecessarily to ambiguity. Communication between people is easily derailed under the best of conditions, so whenever there's a lot riding on getting it right—when we're expressing needs that aren't being met, or setting boundaries, or just saying no—a straightforward approach is the key.

To be fair to Aunt Em, she deserves some credit. She may be stifled, but she does manage to convey disapproval without betraying her sense of propriety. Unfortunately, this isn't enough to stop her neighbor. Being candid might not have worked, either, but its odds of success would have been higher. And Aunt Em would have felt better for it.

10. Stick up for yourself.

Don't expect anyone else to do it (although it's nice when they do). This bit of wisdom is a recurring theme in *The Wizard of Oz*. In Kansas, Aunt Em and Uncle Henry quickly wilt under Miss Gulch's offensive. Dorothy resists, but this first time around she doesn't succeed. Only Toto's resourcefulness in leaping out of Miss Gulch's basket saves him from the fate she has planned for him. In Oz, Dorothy will get another chance to assert herself, with better results.

11. Avoid regrets:
honor your caregivers.

Parents fall short of ideal much of the time. I know I do, and so did my mother and father. Aunt Em and Uncle Henry certainly have their failings, too. However, blaming your caregivers for what's wrong with your life doesn't make things any better. No one comes through childhood unscathed, and as adults it's up to us to make sense of those wounds, to clean them up as best we can, and to put them into perspective. It helps to appreciate that whoever raised us was doing the best they could, even when it wasn't very good. Learn what you can from their mistakes, talk to them about what happened if you can, forgive them, and release what's behind you into the past.

As parents age it's often easier to see the love that lies below the surface. Also, clarity of this kind comes more easily under duress. In Dorothy's case, when she runs away it doesn't take much prompting from Professor Marvel before she recalls Aunt Em's kindness: "I had the measles once, and she stayed right by me every minute." Moments later, Dorothy decides not to visit the crowned heads of Europe with Professor Marvel after all, but to return home instead.

Honor your caregivers. If they're still alive, thank them for everything they have done for you. Coming to appreciate just how much effort, time, money, and love your parents have given you is a way of honoring yourself as well as them. It's also a way of modeling the behavior you'd like to see from your own children when you're old and gray.

12. It's called good luck for a reason.

It's better to be lucky than smart, or so they say. What I know for sure is that good fortune is always welcome in my life, whenever it chooses to make an appearance. When Dorothy packs up her basket and hits the open road with Toto, she catches a break. Where she might have encountered a stranger with dark intentions, instead she comes across the kindhearted Professor Marvel. I must confess that when I'm watching the film these days, my chest still tightens with apprehension when Dorothy lets the silver-tongued carnival fakir lead her into his gloomy caravan. Yet I know there's no need to worry. Professor Marvel may be a flimflam artist, but he steers Dorothy in the right direction: homeward.

AS DOROTHY AND TOTO race back to the Gale farm, the sky darkens ominously. A giant tornado is approaching. While Uncle Henry, Hunk, Hickory, and Zeke loose the horses from the barn, Aunt Em searches frantically for her niece. The tornado is almost upon them when Uncle Henry pulls Aunt Em into the storm cellar, latching the door. Discovering she's locked out, Dorothy makes her way into the house just as the twister hits. A window breaks loose, knocking Dorothy unconscious as the tornado effortlessly lifts up the house and carries it away.

Kansas has set the stage, and the time has come to leave the Sunflower State behind. Now that we know the threats Dorothy is facing, we're heading over the rainbow, where we will discover how they can be resolved.

IN THE LAND OF OZ

We're all fascinated by dreams, and for good reason. Like elves in a fairy tale secretly working on the cobbler's shoes in the wee hours of the night, they offer glimpses of cognitive forces hidden deep inside us, busily sorting things out while we sleep. Greek philosophers placed great significance on dreams, and Sigmund Freud famously used them together with a theory of repressed sexuality to form the basis of modern psychology. His colleague Carl Jung saw dreams as emissaries from the unconscious psyche, that mysterious region of the self that stirs like magma below the crust of our everyday thoughts. This realm, in turn, provides access to our larger collective unconscious, with its universal patterns and images.

According to Joseph Campbell, the unconscious mind is home not just to Jung's archetypes but also to the wellspring of myth. That is certainly the case in *The Wizard of Oz*. Dorothy's dream doesn't echo just any myth, either; it's the greatest myth of all, the classic tale of the Hero's Journey. Every culture has its variations, for this is the story of our common human struggle to individuate, to separate ourselves from our parents and to find our own way. This is the ultimate rite of passage.

Some of us let go of our childish ways more easily than others, but there's no getting around the hero's task. It's a basic requirement of this lifetime, and as we've seen, it's coming for you whether you embrace it or not. In *The Wizard of Oz* Dorothy does an exemplary job of taking on the mantle of adulthood, which is why the film speaks to generations of new viewers, decade after decade. It's the reason we're taking the time to examine the movie so closely, first in Kansas and now in Oz, searching for clues to Dorothy's success that we can borrow to shape our own.

The first insight on this side of the rainbow is deceptively simple. . . .

13. Showing up is at least half the battle.

Allow me to explain. When eventually the tornado weakens, the Gale farmhouse corkscrews to the ground with a big bump, followed by an eerie silence. Before Dorothy even steps out the front door, she has already dramatically shifted the balance of power in Oz. Her house has fallen on the Wicked Witch of the East and crushed her, so now only one wicked witch, her sister, remains. Oz's troubles have just been cut by half! And Munchkinland has been freed from its oppressor, inspiring an ecstatic celebration.

Once again, Dorothy teaches by example. Look how much she has accomplished just by showing up. Literally. Whether it happens by accident or design, showing up is the essential prerequisite for any task worth doing. Being a good parent or friend; succeeding professionally; exercising regularly; participating in the community; practicing a musical instrument: whatever it is you'd like to be or do, you're going to have to show up first.

A higher-order variation on showing up is the focus of our next Emerald of Wisdom, so I won't go into detail here, other than to say that it's more than just a matter of physical attendance. Our attention is required, too. Now when we show up we're fully present. We've resisted the tug of the hyperactive mind, pulling us in a million different directions. We've anchored ourselves in this present moment as it is unfolding, right here and now. This is one of the greatest gifts we can offer to ourselves, as well as to those with whom we're choosing to spend our time.

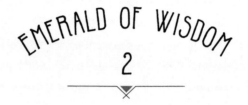

EMERALD OF WISDOM
2

See the world as if for the first time.

"The mind of the beginner is empty, free of the habits of the expert, ready to accept, to doubt, and open to all the possibilities. It is the kind of mind which can see things as they are, which step by step and in a flash can realize the original nature of everything." With these words Zen master Richard Baker could be describing Dorothy's inner state as she opens the farmhouse door and steps from the dull sepia tones of Kansas into the lustrous, Technicolor Land of Oz. Giant flowers sparkle as if coated with glass, a yellow path leads to a bridge across an impossibly blue stream studded with giant lily pads. Nearby steps lead to a spectacular fountain, and beyond that to a cluster of thatched round dwellings. Her face a study in wonder, Dorothy utters the now-immortal line "Toto, I have a feeling we're not in Kansas anymore."

From her very first moment in Oz, Dorothy suspends the natural human tendency to judge her new surroundings. When we find ourselves in unusual circumstances this impulse to judge usually gets amped up, but Dorothy looks around calmly at a world where everything is new and strange. Munchkinland, with its lush flora and plunging cliffs, couldn't be more different from the flat, monochromatic landscape she knows, yet Dorothy greets her new environment with curiosity, not apprehension.

A glowing bubble approaches, lands, and a tall lady steps out, elegantly clad in a sparkly pink gown. *Well, this is interesting.* Deliriously happy crowds of little people wearing flowerpot hats and elfin shoes with curlicue toes suddenly emerge from hiding and begin to sing. *Looks like fun.* A horse-drawn carriage pulls up alongside Dorothy. *I'll step right in.* Dorothy doesn't shrink from anything that's happening, however fantastic it may be. She's not skeptical, dismissive, or fearful—unless there's truly something to fear. She's fully present, wholly open to the experience. In the deeper sense, she's showing up.

Dorothy is the ideal traveler. She greets Oz with that sense of innocence, openness, and wonder Richard Baker describes above, known in Buddhism as Beginner's Mind—the ability to see everything as if for the first time. Typically, we tend to go on automatic pilot in our daily lives and no longer really see what's most familiar: spouses, children, the daily commute to and from work, household chores, the neighborhood in which we live. They dim and go gray. But viewed as if for the first time, the commonplace is suddenly brimming with color and light, alive with possibilities.

From this fresh perspective, take a moment to consider whatever you may be facing. Make a conscious effort to set aside your accumulated memories, biases, or prejudices, and approach the moment with a mental tabula rasa, a blank slate. This skill improves with practice, but even a first-time effort yields results. What assumptions are you bringing to that job interview, that blind date, or that client meeting? How does it look when you set those preconceptions aside? Brighter? Clearer? More enjoyable?

From the moment Dorothy opens that farmhouse door, she is modeling a new way of seeing things, free from the distorted lens of bias. Beginner's Mind is one of the twin pillars of mind-fulness, the meditative awareness that cultivates our capacity to see things just as they are from moment to moment. The other pillar is compassion, which we'll explore later on. Not mired in her own judgments, Dorothy locates herself fully in her experience.

I had a great time working with Nancy Bardacke on her book, *Mindful Birthing*. An experienced nurse practitioner and midwife, Nancy is wise and calm, just the kind of person you'd want with you when a new baby is coming into the world. Twenty years ago she began adapting Jon Kabat-Zinn's mindfulness-based stress reduction program (MBSR) to create the mindfulness-based childhood and parenting program (MBCP), and in *Mindful Birthing* she describes a classic mindfulness exercise, the Raisin Meditation.

Have you tried this? If not, find a place where you can sit quietly. Place a raisin in your hand and leisurely explore it as if you'd never encountered a raisin before, with all your senses. Touch the raisin, smell it, notice its wrinkles and folds, its shades of color. Squeeze it. Take a moment to consider the long journey this raisin has made from the vine to the palm of your hand. When you're ready, slowly place it in your mouth. Feel it with your tongue. Move it around the inside of your mouth. Observe the sudden burst of flavor as you bite into it, and the surge of saliva as you deliberately chew the raisin and finally swallow it. Imagine giving yourself more opportunities to experience the world around you in this mindful way.

This Emerald is an invitation to push the reset button on whatever frame of mind you typically bring to challenging situations. Choose any strategy you find helpful when you need a mental cleanse. Go for a walk, work out, take a bath or swim, meditate, take a nap. Then, when you're ready, imagine yourself as Dorothy after her farmhouse has landed with a thump, opening the door onto a sparkling world unlike anything she's ever seen before.

Become fully aware of being here, in this moment. Feel the air on your skin. Sense the breath moving gently in and out of your nostrils, and the rise and fall of your chest. Tune in to the experience of being alive at this very moment: oxygen, carbon, hydrogen, nitrogen, calcium, and phosphorus have all entered into an unlikely conspiracy to support your existence. You're not in Kansas anymore. You've stepped into Beginner's Mind!

14. Don't be fooled by appearances–and don't take anyone else's word for what they mean.

To settle Dorothy's confusion over how Glinda could possibly be a witch when all witches are old and ugly, Glinda says, "Only bad witches are ugly." This pulled me up short. Is Oz really so different from the world I'm living in? Are things in Oz always what they appear to be on the surface? As we discover later, wizards in Oz are not always what they seem, which tells us that Glinda's rule doesn't apply across the board. So what can we learn here?

Both Dorothy and Glinda are generalizing based on limited experience, which is not the best approach if you're looking for the truth. Dorothy only knows about witches from fairy tales, and Glinda's research is based on a tiny sampling of three (one of whom has just been crushed by a flying farmhouse). Neither Glinda nor Dorothy possesses enough information to arrive at a valid conclusion. The lesson, then, is twofold: *Don't* take people at face value, even when an authority figure says you should. Instead, reserve judgment until you've done some investigating yourself.

This puts me in an awkward position. Here I am, offering you insights from *The Wizard of Oz* while cautioning you not to accept someone else's idea of what qualifies as wisdom and what doesn't. I'm okay with this, actually, and I'll be consistent. Don't accept the Oz insights I'm offering before giving them a test-drive yourself. Balance them against what you know, as well as whatever new information you gather on your own.

Seeing through illusion to the truth, not getting fooled by appearances, is a central theme in *The Wizard of Oz*. Much more on this topic still to come!

EMERALD OF WISDOM
3

Celebrate yourself—and others—for showing up.

Reassured by Glinda's presence and by Dorothy's assertion that she herself is not a witch, the hidden residents of Munchkin City emerge from the bushes to celebrate their new freedom, and to honor Dorothy, their liberator, with songs, gratitude, and a glorious parade. The mayor himself gives Dorothy the keys to the city. She's an instant legend!

Dorothy has done nothing—at least not intentionally—to justify this spectacular welcome, but it provides a wonderful counterbalance to Kansas, where she seems to be constantly underfoot. All she has done here in Oz is arrive, yet by doing so she has killed the Wicked Witch of the East and liberated the Munchkin people. I take this to mean that by showing up we can all be heroes on this journey of life, a fact that deserves to be celebrated. It's far too easy to lose sight of how wondrous life is. Just *being* here is cause for joy (and maybe even a bust in the Munchkin Hall of Fame!).

This festive outpouring in Munchkinland is one of the hallmarks of a rite of passage. Cultures all over the world find ways to mark the transition to adulthood that Dorothy is making. In the case of my own children, who were raised Jewish, bar and bat mitzvahs at age thirteen provided the opportunity for them to be celebrated by their community as they crossed this threshold. I grew up Episcopalian, and at around that same age I received confirmation and took my first communion. Looking back on it, I wish I had understood the significance of that moment more clearly and had made it more cause for celebration, but nevertheless it served its purpose. I felt recognized.

The lesson here has several moving parts. The first is becoming aware that simply by being present we have an impact on other people. Like entangled particles in physics, we affect each other

powerfully in ways that are still only dimly understood. Recognizing that we change things simply
by showing up, whether we want to or not, is the
first step in taking full responsibility for our lives.
When the effect we have on other people is positive, this is cause for celebration. They celebrate
us; we celebrate them; we celebrate ourselves. It's
a way of beginning to accept our inherent power,
another ongoing theme in *The Wizard of Oz*.

Also, celebration strikes me as the opposite of
judgment. Once you stop placing an emphasis on
flaws (your own or someone else's), you're creating
space for a new way of seeing the world. Once you
let go of the mind's tendency to criticize and compare, what's left is appreciation for the beauty of
things as they are. This includes you, so celebrate
yourself. You're awesome!

If you haven't felt this way lately, now is the moment to make up for lost time. Uncork that inner
joy that you've kept stoppered up. Isn't today your
birthday? If not, give yourself permission to act as
if it were. Invite friends over. Make your favorite
dinner. Use the fireplace to make s'mores. You
know what to do. Celebrate responsibly, and with
your whole heart. This is what Dorothy does in her

dream of Oz. From the very outset she's attuned to just how wondrous everything is—and the breathtaking landscape reflects this feeling back to her. As Glinda puts it, "When she fell out of Kansas a miracle occurred."

So, bring on the mayor, the keys to the city, the witty songs in your honor, the horse-drawn carriage, the ecstatic thrill of a parade, and the future bust in the Hall of Fame! If you've ever thought you were a little person in a big people's world, now you see that you were mistaken. You fit right in. This isn't arrogance, or egotism. It's not self-indulgence. It's the simple acknowledgment of a basic truth: being here in this moment, in this transient life, is worthy cause for festivity. Woo-hoo! Now you're ready to embark on your own Yellow Brick Road the same way Dorothy did, with a supercharged boost of self-nourishment.

15. Calmly and clearly is the best way to set boundaries.

Establishing clear personal boundaries is a basic principle when it comes to creating healthy, supportive, and respectful relationships. As a firstborn child and people-pleaser, I, for one, don't come to this easily. I tend to err on the side of avoiding conflict, which can put me in situations where my toes are being stepped on. I've learned from experience that setting boundaries calmly and clearly early on—*this is okay, and this is not*—saves wear and tear all around.

Glinda models both the importance of setting boundaries and a gracious yet effective way to go about it. While the Munchkins and Dorothy are justifiably terrified by the arrival of the Wicked Witch of the West, Glinda keeps her cool and even laughs at her wicked counterpart's threats. "Oh, ho, ho, rubbish. You have no power here. Be gone before somebody drops a house on you, too!" For now, Glinda's unruffled boundary setting has done its work. Dorothy, however, will need to take stronger measures later on.

16. Watch out for houses falling from the sky (especially if you're being wicked).

No explanation needed here. This good advice comes a little late for the Wicked Witch of the East, but it's clearly having an impact on her sister.

17. It's always best to start at the beginning.

After the Wicked Witch of the West departs, Dorothy determines that her best chance of returning to Kansas lies with the great and wonderful Wizard of Oz, who lives in the Emerald City. In response to Dorothy's question about where she should start her journey, Glinda says, "It's always best to start at the beginning," and Dorothy takes this commonsense suggestion very literally. The Yellow Brick Road begins with a spiral that Dorothy could easily cut across, or skip altogether, but she does neither. Carefully she sets her Ruby Slipper right at the very point of the spiral and takes the first steps that will take her out of Munchkinland.

I find Dorothy's approach noteworthy. It leaves me thinking that you and I would do well to take Glinda's suggestion literally, too. Shortcuts can save time, but when the journey is important it's best not to skip any steps or make any assumptions. Take it from the very beginning. One foot in front of the other, that's the best way forward. One moment, one day, at a time.

18. Beginnings are a gift made possible by endings.

I love beginnings and the opportunity they provide to reset and start anew. The first day of school. The first day at a new job. The first light of a new day. However, starting something means leaving something else behind. The leisure of summer gives way to September's classes. The familiar duties of the old job are replaced by a steep learning curve at the new one. Trying something for the first time requires letting go of something familiar. To experience life over the rainbow, Dorothy must leave Kansas behind.

19. When you're lost, it's okay to ask for directions.

My parents made every effort to keep their disagreements out of sight of the children. This made it all the more dramatic each year at Thanksgiving, when my father's stubborn unwillingness to ask for directions to our cousins' house on Long Island led to a series of wrong turns and heated exchanges between my parents. Now that my dad's long gone, I'm the one on car trips who struggles to admit that he might not know which turn to take. Dorothy, however, is blissfully unconstrained by such personal limitations.

She's completely comfortable asking Glinda for directions to the Emerald City, to which Glinda gives her famous answer, "Just follow the Yellow Brick Road." But even when the way forward is obvious, it may not be easy to follow. Fortunately, when Dorothy comes to a crossroads, a talking scarecrow is there to offer guidance. His suggestions are a bit confusing at first, but by stopping to ask for directions our heroine has made a wise decision that will serve her well.

20. Remember your manners.

My mother used to tell me, my brother, and my sister a possibly apocryphal story about the queen of England, as a way of coaxing us to use good table manners. One evening at a formal dinner in the royal palace, a foreign dignitary unaware of Western etiquette drank his finger bowl of rosewater instead of using it to rinse his hands. Alertly recognizing the possibility that he might feel embarrassed, the queen rose to the occasion. Her Highness calmly drained her own rosewater, and once she did so, everyone else followed suit. The purpose of good manners, Mom often reminded us, was first and foremost to make people feel comfortable.

In Oz, after recovering from her surprise at meeting a scarecrow who can speak, Dorothy visibly remembers her manners and starts over again. "Well, we haven't really met properly, have we?" In the exchange that follows, Dorothy learns that the Scarecrow isn't doing at all well: it's terribly tedious being stuck up on that pole all day long. Dorothy offers to help, bends a nail, and the next thing you know, she's found a friend.

Good manners may seem superficial. However, being polite is an essential element of civility, and civility eases the way for new friendships. It also makes it possible for us to disagree while still showing each other respect. In these contentious times, we acutely need this common ground to create dialogue to bridge our differences. *Civilis* is the Latin root of the word *civility* as well as a contributor to *civilization*; without the one, it's difficult to imagine a bright future for the other.

Politeness and civility open the door to kindness. Kindness unlatches the gates of compassion, our next Emerald of Oz.

EMERALD OF WISDOM
4

Choose compassion.

Let's recap briefly. Dorothy's longings have taken her over the rainbow, where she experiences everything as if for the first time, marveling at the beauty of her surroundings and reveling in a surge of celebratory joy. As Dorothy becomes aware of just how wondrous everything is—and how connected she is to it—a new feeling naturally arises from her enlightened state. Almost inevitably, compassion becomes the guiding principle for her actions, smoothing her passage along the Yellow Brick Road.

The Dalai Lama, arguably the most compassionate person on the planet, describes this quality as altruism colored by empathy, an active force dedicated to freeing others from suffering. He believes that compassion contains the power to transform whatever it touches. Like the legendary philosopher's stone, which purportedly allowed alchemists to transmute lead into gold, compassion morphs the people we meet—even enemies—into allies.

Dorothy's consistent application of compassion enhances her travels at every turn. Once she becomes aware that the Scarecrow is uncomfortable on that pole, her immediate response is "let me help you." With a little guidance from the ostensibly brainless Scarecrow, Dorothy sets him free. A stranger in a strange land, Dorothy has just made a new friend who would gladly risk his life for her, should the need arise. And it will, it will.

When Dorothy comes across the Tin Man, rusted solid in the woods, she's quick to apply an oilcan to his frozen joints. On hearing his story, and commiserating with the depths of his plight, she extends the Tin Man an invitation to join her and the Scarecrow on their journey to Emerald City, where perhaps the great Wizard of Oz could give him a heart. Moments later we see Dorothy reap the benefits of this act of loving-kindness. When the Wicked Witch of the West shows up and sets the Scarecrow on fire, the Tin Man courageously uses his metal hat to snuff out the flames. Compassion has brought yet another stalwart to Dorothy's supporting cast.

Her encounter with the Cowardly Lion provides the most dramatic example of the alchemy of compassion. When he comes bounding out of the woods with a fearsome roar and chases Toto, Dorothy protects her dog by stepping up to the Cowardly Lion and giving him a whack on the snout. However, once she realizes that underneath all that bluster the lion is frightened, Dorothy reaches out to comfort him. She not only forgives him, but also includes him in her little band traveling to the Emerald City. In a twinkling the Cowardly Lion, too, becomes a loyal ally.

Of the various cases the Dalai Lama makes on behalf of compassion, two in particular appeal to me. The first is based on the Buddhist principle of reincarnation. If we're endlessly born into new lives after we die, the Dalai Lama says, then anyone we meet might have been responsible for nurturing us as infants in the past, or could do so in the future. People, animals, birds: any living being might be your potential parent, aunt, uncle, or grandparent. (I'm reminded of the ditty "Be kind to your web-footed friends, for that duck could be somebody's mother.") So how could you not greet every living thing with filial respect and affection?

Second, the Dalai Lama argues that during the first few years of our lives we're completely reliant on the kindness of others for food, shelter, affection, and diapering. This is also true at the end of our lives, if we're lucky enough to reach old age. Therefore, shouldn't we be paying that childhood kindness forward during the middle part of our lives, while we're still capable of taking care of other people? What a beautifully pragmatic perspective! Viewed in these ways, the world bends toward compassion.

Have you ever wondered why your dog, or that bird at the bird feeder, or the stranger walking ahead of you on the street, suddenly stops to return your gaze? Physicists and spiritual sages will tell you that it's because at some basic level we're all connected. One way of putting this awareness to good use is through a loving-kindness meditation. While sitting quietly with your eyes closed, focus your attention on someone who strongly evokes in you a feeling of love and compassion. This could be a spouse, or a child, a relative, or a close friend. Then consciously extend this circle of love outward. Include more friends and family members, and then your larger community. Now expand those ripples of compassion ever more widely to include everyone in your region, your state, your country, and the world. Farther and farther out they go, until your loving-kindness encompasses the entire universe.

We have no indication that Dorothy used this particular practice, yet her behavior in Oz consistently reflects kindness. Even the moment when she destroys her nemesis, the Wicked Witch of the West, springs from a compassionate impulse to help the Scarecrow. You could even make the argument that the powerful magic of the Ruby Slippers is only available to Dorothy because she has walked so many miles of the Yellow Brick Road in someone else's shoes! Over and over again, compassion transmutes the raw materials of Oz in ways that make Dorothy's journey such a golden success.

The Land of Oz, you'll notice, is not transactional. In the film Dorothy never pays for anything, not for that cab ride or that visit to the beautician. In Baum's book she's offered food and drink and lodging along the Yellow Brick Road, yet money never changes hands. Oz is utopian in a way that the world we're living in is not, and one message

Dorothy's dream conveys is that deep within each of us we aspire to such generosity. In what way—small as a smile or big as a squirt of oil on a rusty stranger—can you and I help bring this aspect of Oz to life?

21. Helping others gives you a boost, too.

When it comes to our ongoing quest to understand what makes us tick, the fight-or-flight response may grab the headlines, but we human beings are hard-wired to do more than just protect ourselves. For one thing, oxytocin, the love hormone released by the brain, plays an essential role in social connections, in sexuality, and in bonding before and after childbirth. For another, our ability to survive as a species is based on cooperation. Alone, we were easy prey; together, we've dominated the planet.

In a world where *getting* receives so much airtime, it turns out that *giving* is the only way to meet one of our deepest needs: the desire to belong, which Dorothy expresses so passionately in "Over the Rainbow." Social psychology shows that when we greet other people with compassion, we also lower our own levels of stress, distrust, and loneliness. Compassion is both selfless and selfish at the same time; by doing good for others, we do well by ourselves.

22. As you see the world, so it shall be.

As the Cowardly Lion bears witness, our experience of life is shaped by what we believe. If I think the world is a scary place, then for me it's going to be frightening. When I establish a conscious belief about how things work, I'm going to look for evidence to support it (just look at all those terrible events in the news!), and even behave in ways that reinforce it. Acting fearful, for example, tends to bring out the aggressor in other people, whereas acting assertively can have the opposite effect. If I believe most people are helpful and friendly, then that's how they're going to show up for me.

Every now and then I like to confirm this hypothesis by testing it. When I see someone on the street or in the supermarket or the gym who looks grumpy or even intimidating, I'll go out of my way to say hello. It's amazing how often even the most hostile-looking person will respond with a friendly greeting, or brighten that scowling face with a companionable grin. As the famous saying goes, "Be the change you want to see in the world." When you greet the world with a smile, the world smiles back.

23. We're not the best judges of ourselves.

From Dorothy's very first encounter with the Scarecrow on the Yellow Brick Road, this insight is beautifully and bountifully conveyed. We'll explore its implications in the next Emerald, but for now we can find ample evidence of our inability to accurately assess our strengths and weaknesses in the Scarecrow, the Tin Man, and the Cowardly Lion. The first is certain he has no brains. The second thumps his hollow chest, convinced that he has no heart. The third feels shame for his lack of courage. Yet time and again events in Oz demonstrate that these self-assessments fly well wide of the mark. In fact, if Dorothy's companions are any indication, this inaccuracy is so jaw

dropping that it may point the way to a related insight. . . .

24. When it comes to assessing ourselves, we may be getting it completely butt-backwards.

Think you're brainless? Truth is, you're probably witty, insightful, and resourceful. Think you have no feelings? You're likely brimming over with sensitivity. Think you're a coward? You're probably brave enough to be king of the forest. As *The Wizard of Oz* so dra-matically illustrates, we all may be seeing ourselves in wildly inaccurate ways. When we behave accordingly we can end up moving further and further from what really matters. This is why the next Emerald of Wis-dom is such a game changer.

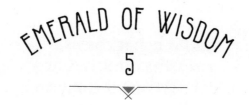

EMERALD OF WISDOM
5

You already possess what you desire most.

When Dorothy first meets the Scarecrow, the Tin Man, and the Cowardly Lion, they're stuck, snared by mistaken beliefs about themselves. Part of what makes *The Wizard of Oz* so enjoyable, especially for children, is just how obvious this is. By pointing out that some people who talk a lot haven't got any brains at all, the Scarecrow establishes how clever he is in his very first exchange with Dorothy. With every facial gesture and dramatic observation, the Tin Man makes it abundantly clear that his ostensibly hollow chest is actually crammed full of feelings. And the Cowardly Lion's cowardice is so preposterous that his quest for courage seems laughable. How can these three characters not see what is so obvious to the rest of us? The absurdity of the situation makes it so highly entertaining, yet its message is nonetheless profound.

This fifth Emerald of Wisdom provides an antidote to self-doubt and to misconceptions about ourselves that often play such an outsize role in our lives. They can keep us stuck on a pole, or frozen with rust. Derailed by mistaken beliefs about ourselves, we can lose sight of what's obvious to any casual observer. We clutch at straws, we travel with oilcans, we can't sleep for fear of the sheep we're counting. We get things completely backwards. We don't realize that we already possess what matters most to us, and in the process, we lose sight of who we are.

To free ourselves from these illusions, let's begin by identifying what matters most—both in the film and in our own lives. No surprise here. It's precisely those qualities represented by the Scarecrow, the Tin Man, and the Cowardly Lion. Wisdom. Heart. Courage. The first of these helps us make good choices, learn from our mistakes, and become increasingly aware of what really matters in life. The second helps us sift through a maelstrom of feelings so we can employ them in service of those emotions that matter most—love and compassion. Lastly, courage allows us to act in the face of fear, to feel that fear and do it anyway.

The next step is to understand that, despite our doubts, we already possess all three of these all-important qualities. Not sure? Think about it for a moment. You're reading these words because you appreciate the value of wisdom, and it's just not possible to value a quality that you don't already own. You wouldn't know what wisdom was, much less want more of it.

The same is true of heart. You may find it difficult to get in touch with your feelings sometimes, or they may overwhelm you, but there's no doubt that you're endowed with them. You are in full possession of what we commonly describe as the seat of our emotions, the heart. Learning to respect your emotions, to listen to them while at the same time appreciating that they can change as easily as the thoughts that trigger them, is part of becoming skilled in the ways of the heart. Just as you can become wiser, you can also become more adept with your emotions, more capable of loving and being loved.

As far as courage goes, you've got that in abundance, too. As humans we're uniquely aware of just how brief this lifetime is, yet we overcome the fears associated with that awareness dozens of times each day, beginning with getting out of bed in the morning. And like brains and heart, the more you acknowledge that courage, the more it makes itself known.

Because they emanate from Dorothy's dream, the Scarecrow, Tin Man, and Cowardly Lion also represent Dorothy's own need to recognize and befriend her brains, heart, and courage. All three have been called into question. In Kansas, Hunk tells Dorothy she isn't using her head when she continues to walk past Miss Gulch's house: "Think you didn't have any brains at all!" Aunt Em points out the volatility of Dorothy's emotions, accusing her of always getting herself "into a fret over nothing." And Dorothy's courage has been tested by Miss Gulch's frontal assault. Just as her three friends eventually come to realize that they possess what they've always longed for, so does Dorothy. And as she does, so do we.

Self-doubts and misconceptions will arise on your Yellow Brick Road, and when they do, follow Dorothy's lead. Greet them with compassion, befriend them, and watch those misguided beliefs morph into self-awareness. You already possess what you desire most.

25. The best things in life are free.

Suspended inside the fifth Emerald lies another insight, its inverse. If you already possess what you desire most, then whatever you truly long for cannot lie beyond your reach. This means that what you truly long for can't be money that isn't already in your bank account, or that new car on the showroom floor, or a new home that's not currently in your name. There's no denying these things could make life easier, but this Emerald of Wisdom still holds true. All those classic songs confirm it: the best things in life are free, and money can't buy me love.

We human beings have a natural tendency to compare ourselves to other people. This triggers a lot of unhappiness. In one famous behavioral economics experiment, subjects were asked to choose between earning $50,000 per year while others earned $25,000, or earning $100,000 while others earned $250,000 (the cost of goods and services to remain the same). Study subjects consistently chose the former, even though it was half as much money, just to elevate themselves in relation to others!

The solution? Fight the impulse to look around

in order to see how well you're doing. You've got the power to choose between focusing on what you lack or focusing on what you've got. Choosing the latter would have saved the Scarecrow, the Tin Man, and the Cowardly Lion a long journey, but that's what they needed to do in order to learn this lesson. With any luck, reading this may save you the trip!

26. Keep an eye out for the law of unintended consequences.

Here's a good example of this law in action: by bullying the Scarecrow and the Tin Man, the Wicked Witch of the West only hardens their resolve to help Dorothy. Being aware of the law of unintended consequences is a good general principle. At a minimum it keeps you humble, and we'll see how valuable that can be. It can also inspire you to think things through more carefully, to consider the ramifications of that chess move a few steps beyond where you've been content to stop. This is the road to becoming a master. Keeping an eye out for the law of unintended consequences is a great way to up your game.

27. You can face anything when you're arm in arm with friends.

We humans are social by nature. We may enjoy being alone sometimes, but we're hardwired for community; everything goes better when our arms are intertwined—even the moments when we're most afraid. Lions and tigers and bears, oh my!

High on my bucket list is spending more time with good friends. Those moments together feel like stepping into comfortable old shoes, their easy fit shaped by years of intimate contact. Whenever I'm blue, or frustrated, or grumpy, calling an old friend and having a long talk, or getting together for a meal, restores my good spirits every time.

When she lands in Oz, Dorothy has no friends but Toto, yet by the time she leaves she has three great ones. Lessons emerge from how she makes those friends, yet what we take away from the unforgettable image where they're singing "We're Off to See the Wizard" is simply how good it is to share good times—or bad—with people we enjoy and trust. There's nothing like it.

28. Skipping is always a quick pick-me-up.

When was the last time you skipped down the road, with or without friends? May I suggest that it's been too long? Skipping comes more naturally for children, so we have to make more of a conscious effort as adults. But even the attempt is good for a laugh.

29. You can't laugh and be afraid at the same time.

Laughter is the one thing fear cannot abide. The Cowardly Lion is so hilarious that viewers can't help but laugh at his fears—and in the process they banish their own. It's a valuable lesson, conveyed as an experience rather than as a moral, both in Frank Baum's book and the movie it inspired.

Slapstick humor and joyful punning are elevated to high art in *The Wizard of Oz*, and Bert Lahr as the Cowardly Lion is its consummate practitioner. Because he's so funny, the Cowardly Lion leads us to doubt that he's really as scared as he says he is. How could he be, when he tells us he can't fall asleep by counting sheep because he's "afraid of 'em"?

30. Fear is nothing to be ashamed of.

"Wouldn't you feel degraded to be seen in the company of a cowardly lion? I would," sobs the king of the beasts. Although fear can be a lifesaver, when it becomes chronic it can become debilitating. Hiding those terrors away because they're shameful only makes things worse. The cure is to bring them into the light, which the Cowardly Lion does without need for much prompting. "My life has been simply unbearable," he tells Dorothy. "It's been in me so long, I just gotta tell ya how I feel."

Once we work up the courage to share what scares us with other people, we can begin to shrink those fears down to manageable size. We're both removing the destructive element of shame that the Cowardly Lion just referred to, and we're using fear to create connections with each other, to build a community of people who understand what we're going through. Speaking for myself, I know that generally I feel much closer to people who are willing to discuss their fears and insecurities, who have the courage to reveal those parts of themselves that don't merit applause or medals. It's how we really get to know each other.

31. Don't be seduced by pretty poppies.

Shame, fear, and pain are so difficult to manage that sometimes numbing ourselves seems like an irresistible solution. What's worse, this strategy often comes seductively packaged, whether it's that colorful container of ice cream, a glowing bottle of aged whiskey, or the languorous beauty of an opioid dream. That's what makes the Wicked Witch of the West's next move so diabolical: a magic spell to conjure up something "with poison in it, but attractive to the eye and soothing to the smell." Poppies.

When Dorothy and her companions reach the outskirts of Emerald City, she's delighted by the breathtaking fields of bright red flowers. But joy gives way to sudden fatigue; she and Toto and the Cowardly Lion collapse and can't be wakened. Take a tip from their experience. If you fall asleep in a poppy field, you're in mortal danger. That bower of crimson petals may look appealing, but there are wicked forces at work.

Wake up! And if it's too late to rouse yourself from the poppies' seductive beauty, perhaps your friends can draw on their brains, heart, and courage to help. They may need to call on the higher power that Glinda represents in order to prevail, but fortunately the Scarecrow and Tin Man prove resourceful enough to do just that.

When it comes to addiction, I've always struggled with food. After trying Weight Watchers with initial success but diminishing returns, I learned about an outpatient program for eating disorders at the University of North Carolina. It involved group therapy as well as reading assignments like the work of Brené Brown. In her popular TED Talk and various books, Brown zeroes in on topics the rest of us would rather not discuss: vulnerability, authenticity, connection, and shame. Geneen Roth does much the same thing.

In a nutshell, this work involves becoming aware that food will never fill that emotional void we're stuffing it with, and that shame perpetuates a destructive cycle of bingeing and regret. Group therapy makes it possible to explore the feelings we hide even from ourselves, and to find out that they're not as terrible as we think they are, nor as unique. (Good friends can help with this, too.) Lo and behold, when you name your shame like the Cowardly Lion does, it loses a lot of its power. When your fellow patients name theirs, the stage is set for healing: sleeping forever in a field of poppies, or getting to the bottom of that gallon of ice cream, starts to lose its appeal.

32. When you ask for help, don't be shy: shout at the top of your lungs!

I love the moment in *The Wizard of Oz* right after Dorothy, Toto, and the Cowardly Lion have keeled over in the Deadly Poppy Field. The Scarecrow is admonishing the panicky Tin Man, "It's no use screaming at a time like this! Nobody will hear you!" But then with his very next breath the Scarecrow begins to shout, "HELP! HELP! HELP!"

When people you love are in trouble, it's no time to be tentative. When your own need is great, it's no time to be shy. Call for help and let the world know you mean it. Don't whisper, SHOUT!

They say that preachers and rabbis give the sermons they need to hear. The same must be true of authors, since so many of these insights from Oz speak to issues in my own life. I've always been reluctant to ask for help, or to accept it when offered. I've viewed need as a sign of weakness, and weakness as something to hide. But as I get older, and perhaps a little wiser, I'm coming to see asking for help as a sign of strength.

33. When you need to, call in support from a higher power.

This one is easier for me, perhaps because I can make this request privately. Still, it requires winning a struggle with my belief that I should be able to do it myself, whatever "it" is. My friend Gerry is a big believer in angels, but he tells me that they have an unusual limitation: they can't work their magic in your life without an invitation. They need your permission to cross the threshold. This may be a basic requirement to activate any intervention from a higher power. It's certainly part of the twelve-step program in AA, and a big reason why people pray!

The Scarecrow may not have had all this in mind when he called out for help in the field of poppies, but his cries worked anyway. Glinda responds to the call for help by using her magic powers to create snow, bringing Dorothy, Toto, and the Cowardly Lion out of their otherwise endless sleep.

34. If you're laughing away every day, there's more going on than meets the eye.

Even after watching *The Wizard of Oz* countless times, I'm not quite sure what to make of the citizens of Emerald City. They profess to be a carefree lot—waking at noon, starting work at one, and knocking off an hour later—but why are they trying so hard to convince us how happy they are? And what are they doing with all those idle hours? Slipping out to cultivate the poppy fields?

All that good cheer certainly rests on a shaky foundation. When the Wicked Witch of the West starts skywriting, residents jettison their jolliness and swarm the gates to the Wizard's palace, clamoring for explanations and reassurance. They're turned away by that familiar-looking guard. "Nobody can see the Great Oz, not nobody, not nohow!"

Residence in Emerald City suddenly loses its luster. All that cheeriness starts to look like whistling in the dark. Once again, things are not always what they appear to be. And when they look too good to be true, they probably are.

35. What makes the muskrat guard his musk? And the Hottentot so hot? Courage!

In Oz we've learned from Dorothy's friends that courage is one of the big three, an essential quality along with brains and heart. With courage you're not just whistling in the dark; you've also got what it takes to face what you find there, a theme we'll explore in the next Emerald.

As a child I was fascinated by conventional tales of bravery, so Stephen Crane's *The Red Badge of Courage* came at me sideways. The book's protagonist, Henry Fleming, wasn't anything like the heroic figures I'd read about in other books. Young and scrawny, he enlists as a private in the Union Army because his head is full of the same dreams of heroism that populated mine as a child. When his unit gets decimated by enemy gunfire, however, he breaks ranks and flees.

Goaded by shame, young Henry returns to the fray and ends up carrying his regimental flag into battle, leading his fellow soldiers on. Still, the novel ends on an ambiguous note. I came away from it with a new understanding of the nature of courage, which is re-inforced by the Wizard of Oz himself at the end of the film. He tells the Cowardly Lion, "You are under the unfortunate delusion that simply because you run away from danger, you have no courage. You're con-fusing courage with wisdom."

The impulse to flee danger is natural, even desir-able in most cases. When it's not—when you have a strong enough reason to overcome those fears—this is when courage comes in. Courage is the qual-ity that makes it possible to feel the fear and do it anyway. Without that manual override we'd be help-less in the face of terrors real and imagined. With it, we're capable of doing what must be done. Muskrats, prepare to guard that musk!

36. If you're truly unhappy, have a good cry.

You'll feel better, which is all the reason any of us needs. And who knows? You might even soften that palace guard's heart the way Dorothy's tears do—so that he changes his mind and grants you an audience with the Great Oz.

37. Revisit a neglected virtue: humility.

Whatever happened to humility? Once a highly regarded virtue, it's almost completely overlooked in this age of branding and self-promotion. Through her actions, though, Dorothy makes a case for reevaluating this unassuming quality. The self-proclaimed Great and Powerful Oz doesn't inspire much confidence, but Dorothy, who bills herself as small and meek, does. She doesn't let success go to her head, and when it's crunch time she shows up in a big way.

Not to be confused with low self-esteem, humility contains a sense of our own value; it's just not over-inflated. Humility is the virtue that encourages us to accept how much we don't know and promotes the importance of listening to others. It makes room for learning, offering a path to wisdom.

The Wizard may not be impressed by humility, but he turns out to be no one to emulate. Dorothy, however, is well served by it. She meets her own needs while still making sure everyone in her small band of fellow travelers gets their needs met, too. Her role in the film also has a real-life parallel. Judy Garland made no attempt to upstage the Scarecrow, the Tin Man, or the Cowardly Lion; instead, she made room for a cast of equals while remaining the movie's undeniable star.

EMERALD OF WISDOM
6

Face what you fear.

With no choice but to perform a "very small task" for the Wizard of Oz in return for his promise to grant their requests, Dorothy and her companions travel into the Haunted Forest. They're on their way to confront Dorothy's terrifying, cackling archenemy and return with her broomstick for the Wizard. Undertaking this journey is an accomplishment in itself, a sign of Dorothy's growing self-assurance, since by all indications it's a suicide mission. Trapped in the witch's castle, surrounded by her Winkie guards, Dorothy and company are bracing for the end when the Wicked Witch of the West touches a burning broom to the Scarecrow's arm, setting it on fire. Desperate to save her companion, Dorothy reaches for a nearby bucket of water and hurls it toward him.

As right action and good luck would have it, enough water lands on the Scarecrow's arm to douse the flames, but most of it splashes on the witch herself. To the astonishment of viewers everywhere, she begins to dissolve, cursing the good little girl who has destroyed her beautiful wickedness. Then, with all the suddenness of her dramatic arrivals, the Wicked Witch of the West melts into a seething heap of clothes topped by her signature conical hat. She is no more. In the end it was simply water, that ubiquitous, fundamental requirement for life, that proved her undoing.

Dorothy faces a daunting fear and it melts away, as fears tend to do when confronted directly. Celebration all around! But as is so often the case with this film, there's more going on beneath the surface.

At first, I assumed this was the moment when Dorothy confronted her greatest fear, but I've come to see it a little differently. It's an uplifting teaching moment, no doubt, however it won't be until the very end of the film that Dorothy faces off against her most daunting challenge. In fact, here in the witch's castle, it's that still unresolved terror that motivates Dorothy to take on the seemingly hopeless quest to kill the Wicked Witch of the West and bring her broomstick back to the Wizard.

What does Dorothy fear more than the Wicked Witch of the West? We find out in the witch's dungeon, when Dorothy looks into the green crone's crystal ball and sees Aunt Em searching for her. More than anything, Dorothy fears losing her aunt. In Kansas, this led Dorothy to return home after running away. In Oz, the threat of losing Aunt Em motivates Dorothy to take on the Wicked Witch of the West, if that's what's required to get home. In this instance, fear serves a valuable purpose.

Fear has always played an outsize role in my life, rooted in my brush with death as a toddler when I contracted polio. In addition to some physical limitations, the disease left me with the kinds of distorted beliefs that we're all prone to acquire in the absence of good information, children most of all. For years I struggled—and sometimes still do— with the conviction that there's something wrong with me, that the two-year-old inside me is still toxic with contagion.

I've since come to realize that we all grapple with variations on this theme of unworthiness. At some point our parents were unable to meet our needs, and being totally dependent on them it was too scary to consider that they might not come through. It was easier to assume we had done something wrong and then strive to correct it, keeping ourselves in the driver's seat even if it meant assigning fault where there was none. Illusion: it's powerful stuff.

My own greatest fear is that lying on my deathbed I'll realize that I've allowed mistaken beliefs formed during childhood to keep me from living fully. It's the worst fate I can imagine. So like Dorothy I use that fear to keep from being hemmed in by lesser frights that go bump in the night; I use it to push myself to do things that otherwise would be too scary.

There's yet another interesting angle to explore here. Sigmund Freud, father of psychoanalysis, believes that behind every fear lies a wish. If Dorothy fears the loss of Aunt Em, this is where we must also look to find the wish: independence from her aunt. Now we've discovered a hidden wellspring of dramatic tension in *The Wizard of Oz*, the clash between two fundamental human needs: to stay home, where you're safe and loved, and to leave that home in order to make a life of your own.

The arrival of Miss Gulch and the inability of Aunt Em and Uncle Henry to protect Toto brings that tension to a boil. Dorothy runs away in order to keep Toto safe, but she isn't yet ready to leave home for good. Still, events in her life keep signaling that it's time for a change. It's particularly telling that Dorothy returns home only to find the cellar door locked, with Aunt Em and Uncle Henry on the other side, unable to hear her cries for help. Despite her reluctance, the locus of agency is shifting to Dorothy. She alone will be able to resolve her competing needs for safety and belonging on the one hand, and for freedom on the other. To do so she must face her fears.

38. If you come across a sign that reads HAUNTED FOREST I'D TURN BACK IF I WERE YOU, now is the time for that courage you've heard so much about!

This moment in the story provides a special opportunity for the Cowardly Lion to show that he's got the right stuff to become king of the forest. As we've seen in his endearing musical performance on the steps in front of the Wizard's palace, the Cowardly Lion has imagined this ascendant moment in great detail, from the regal satin robes he'll wear to the thrashing of a hippopotamus "from top to bottomus," if necessary. Now, as the castle of the Wicked Witch of the West grows closer, he'll get a chance to exercise more than his musical and comedic chops. It's time to show his mettle, and he does.

39. When the sky blackens with Winged Monkeys, RUN!

☺

40. A good leader keeps a light hand on the reins of power.

When the Winged Monkeys capture Dorothy and Toto and fly them to the witch's castle, the Scarecrow, the Tin Man, and the Cowardly Lion are overrun and left behind. They patch themselves together and make their way toward the witch's castle in an effort to rescue Dorothy, each contributing a particular strength to cover the vulnerability of the others. What they use, in a word, is teamwork.

In many ways Dorothy has assembled a remarkable crew whose merits begin with their leader. As we've seen, she is that precious rarity, a principal who doesn't always need to take center stage. On the Yellow Brick Road she consults team members before taking on new additions, and she's fiercely protective once they come on board, standing up for her people whether they're being screamed at by wizards or set ablaze by witches.

In Frank Baum's book there are many additional examples of this teamwork, but perhaps the most dramatic can be found in the way each member steps up to save the group on the way to the witch's castle. The Tin Man, whose metal body is impervious to teeth, uses his ax to chop up a pack of wolves. The Scarecrow, whose painted eyes are not susceptible to a flock of murderous crows, destroys them before they can reach his friends. And the Cowardly Lion roars so fiercely that the witch's army of Winkie soldiers runs away in fright. Only when the Wicked Witch of the West summons the Winged Monkeys does she carry the day. And that triumph, as we know, is only temporary.

41. Being afraid of fear only makes it worse, so befriend it instead.

Fear is a hydra, a multiheaded monster springing from the same mythic depths that gave rise to Oz. One thing that makes this demon so resilient is that we can't take a broadsword and hack it out of our lives. It's hardwired in us, and with good reason. Faced with a real threat, we depend on that fight-or-flight response to kick in, on that rush of adrenaline to give us additional strength, and on that vasoconstriction shunting blood away from the surface and toward our vital organs. We need fear, yet it's a visitor that tends to take up residence uninvited. The trick is to direct it, instead of having it rule our lives.

Where do you feel fear in your body? My chest gets tight, and I feel like I can't breathe. This makes me more upset, until I remind myself how often I've been here before. As a veteran of anxiety, I can offer a few strategies that work for me. First is square breathing. Perform each step to a slow count of four: breathe in: hold; breath out: hold. Repeat as needed. Three or four cycles are usually enough to break fear's irrational grip.

The second approach begins with a careful eval-

uation of my surroundings—the people, any places
hidden from view, the temperature, and any smells or
sounds. Is there a threat now, in this moment? Do I
have any reason to be afraid, above and beyond the
everyday uncertainty we all live with? If the answer is
no, as it almost always is, then I address my anxiety
directly. *I appreciate your desire to protect me. Thank
you. I'm grateful for your speedy arrival, too, but now
that I've checked out the situation, I'm good. No further
cause for concern. Your work here is done.* Then I take a
few deep breaths, and while I'm waiting for my heart
rate to slow, I'll open a book, listen to some music,
start fooling around on my guitar, or otherwise distract myself until my body returns to normal.

In the rare instance when the answer is yes, there is
cause for concern, I prepare to take action. Where is
the nearest exit? Who might need my help? How can
I prepare to manage the situation? Years ago, I earned
my certification as an emergency medical technician,
and volunteered on the local rescue squad. This was
my way of facing my fears. It was also one of the best
decisions I ever made. Now when trouble comes, I'm
looking to see how I can contribute, which helps keep
me from worrying about myself.

As the famous paraphrase of Franklin Delano Roo-
sevelt goes, we have nothing to fear but fear itself, and

most of the time this is true. Dorothy doesn't worry unnecessarily. When her fears arise, they're justified. The situation in the witch's castle is challenging, but she hasn't made it worse. She weeps and calls on Aunt Em for help, but when her friends arrive Dorothy's ready to take action. Once you're no longer afraid of it, fear returns to its function as an early-warning system. Now it's a tool to be used when you need it.

42. Killing with kindness actually works.

Compassion may not come with all the glitzy trappings of magic spells, clouds of smoke, flying monkeys, and terrified subjects, but it's effective. An enemy dissolves thanks to Dorothy's reflexive impulse to protect a friend. A simple bucket of water proves anathema to the Wicked Witch of the West. When your motives are pure—and what could be purer than compassion?—events have a way of supporting you. In the Eightfold Path to enlightenment taught by the Buddha, the fourth aspect of the path is right conduct. We act in this way, without selfish attachment to our own benefit, by being mindful.

43. Consider the possibility that inside every Winkie guard brandishing his wicked spear resides a fearful person waiting for someone courageous enough to set him free.

While Dorothy is showing us a way of being in the world that we can learn from and emulate, the Winkie guards working for the Wicked Witch of the West have something to teach us, too. A power greater than their own has enslaved them to the Wicked Witch of the West, forcing them to do her bidding. Then one day a courageous girl comes along and finds a way to erase the terrible threat hanging over their heads. Moments later the leader of the fearsome Winkie guards turns to Dorothy and swears his allegiance: "Hail to Dorothy! The Wicked Witch is dead!"

What stands revealed is the fundamental goodness of the witch's guards, which until this moment has been shrouded in terror—theirs and ours. Winkies are people just like the rest of us. They love their families. They want to live in peace. They want to treat their neighbors with compassion and to be treated the same way themselves. Unfortunately, they've had to suppress these desires until now.

Not everyone will support you in acting with courage and compassion, but you may find help in surprising places. People want to do the right thing, but they can get tangled up along the way, and even end up acting in service of a witch who takes pleasure in her wickedness. Yet given a chance at a new start, they may well take it, which is one more reason to face your fears. Inside every Winkie warrior you might find a person like you, just trapped by circumstances and waiting to be set free.

44. Even Winged Monkeys have a backstory that makes them less frightening.

For the most part in these pages I've kept our focus on the movie of *The Wizard of Oz*, but occasionally it's helpful to turn to Frank Baum's novel in order to fill in some background that informed the filmmakers, even if it didn't make its way into the movie itself.

In the movie the terrifying Winged Monkeys seem to be one more indication that the powers of darkness vastly outweigh the powers of light, but the full story is less daunting. In his book Baum tells us the witch's control over the Winged Monkeys is only temporary. It's located in a Golden Cap, and whoever wears it can make three wishes, which the monkeys must obey. The story behind this unusual arrangement is told to Dorothy by the leader of the Winged Monkeys in chapter fourteen of *The Wonderful Wizard of Oz*.

Once upon a time the Winged Monkeys were a free people, happy and carefree if a bit too mischievous. A beautiful princess in Oz who also happened to be a powerful sorceress was betrothed to a handsome young man, whom she loved very deeply. Just before their wedding, the young man was strolling along the river in his silk finery when the king of the Winged Monkeys and his band decided to play a prank. They picked him up and dropped him in the river, ruining his clothes. Being a good-natured fellow, he didn't mind, but his bride-to-be was not so kindly disposed. She only refrained from drowning the Winged Monkeys in that same river when they agreed to do the bidding of whoever is wearing the Golden Cap.

Knowledge is power, and in this case knowing the story of the Winged Monkeys helps us see their role as minions of the Wicked Witch of the West in a new light. Like the Winkies their scariness is shaped by circumstance; in this case their power can serve good as well as wickedness, depending on who's wearing the Golden Cap. Just as it's harder to hate someone once you know what they've lived through, it's also more difficult to be frightened by them once you know the full story.

45. Whether or not we keep our promises says a lot about who we are.

I'm not as good about keeping my word as I'd like to be, although I'm working hard to remedy this short-coming. Counting on someone to do as they say is the bedrock of trust. When someone dependable says they've got your back, you can rest easy. When they say they don't, you know to make other plans. Not being sure if they're as good as their word, that's when things become difficult.

Dorothy gets it. Now that she and her companions have successfully returned to Emerald City with the broomstick of the Wicked Witch of the West, Oz begins hemming and hawing about keeping his end of the bargain. This time Dorothy is not the least bit intimidated. "If you were really great and powerful, you'd keep your promises!" Amen to that.

46. Anger has a silver lining.

Can you imagine a Grimms' fairy tale in which a child openly displays anger and gets rewarded for it? I can't, yet that's exactly what happens in *The Wizard of Oz*. Kindness may be Dorothy's default setting, but there are crucial moments when it's her anger that saves the day. She uses it to stand up to the Cowardly Lion when he attacks Toto, and to the Wizard when he tries to wiggle out of his obligations.

Dorothy's anger isn't unbridled, destructive rage. It's a controlled response that stiffens her backbone and helps her speak truth to power, especially in defense of the weak and vulnerable. Dorothy's anger is a legitimate response to injustice, a form of protection that can be extended to those we love. It's righteous anger in the best sense of the term. It's intended not to do harm, but to prevent harm from being done.

EMERALD OF WISDOM
7

**Pull back the curtain and
see things as they really are.**

When Toto pulls back a curtain in the Wizard's magnificent throne room, an imposter stands revealed. A white-haired man is busily pulling levers and speaking into a microphone to create the illusion of the Great and Powerful Oz. When he admits to being a humbug, Dorothy and her companions are angry and disappointed. What about the promises the Wizard has made to provide them with brains, heart, courage—and transportation home?

Happily for the Scarecrow, the Tin Man, and the Cowardly Lion, the Wizard's homilies and ceremonial gifts succeed in bridging their last remaining gaps between self-doubt and truth. Dorothy, however, poses a more significant challenge. To get her home, the Wizard decides to transport Dorothy himself, in the same hot-air balloon that accidentally carried him to Oz many years earlier. However, through a mix of circumstance and incompetence, the Wizard will leave Dorothy stranded at the last moment.

Once again Dorothy must reckon with the painful reality that her trust in authority figures is misplaced. Despite appearances and claims to the contrary, these grown-ups are not larger than life; they don't possess unlimited powers. They don't even have her best interests at heart, at least not reliably. It's a hard lesson, but she's taking it in and coming to terms with the implications: she cannot give her power away. She has to step up, grasp the tiller, and set the course for her own life.

As we're learning from Oz and from Dorothy, we each have to learn how to make our own way. Yes, friends can help, but no one else can decide which path we take. Beware the impulse to give up your messy Technicolor freedom for a consistently green Emerald City. Its residents have made a Faustian bargain!

In a later Emerald of Wisdom, we'll explore the value of placing your faith in something greater than yourself, but not in *someone* greater than yourself. At this point in the story, however, the lesson is clear: don't pin your hopes on another person to show you the way and to take you there—especially if that person presents as all-powerful, paternalistic, and wizardly. Place that faith in yourself, first and foremost. Yes, there's a chance the former approach could turn out okay, but more likely you'll be setting yourself up for massive disappointment. Just ask Dorothy. Or those investors who turned their life savings over to the Professor Marvel of finance, avuncular Bernie Madoff.

Skillful con men have a knack for showing us exactly what we want to see, while out of sight behind the curtain lies something altogether different. Sadly, when the time comes to take that trip back to Kansas—or to draw down those retirement funds—the great and powerful can turn out to be humbugs. The silver lining here in Oz is that Dorothy rises to the occasion by becoming increasingly self-reliant.

In the world of this film women are the primary power holders, which contributes to Dorothy's maturation. From the moment she steps into the Land of Oz, she's presumed to be a major player.

Glinda's first question of Dorothy is, "Are you a good witch or a bad witch?" Even after Dorothy's categorical denial, Glinda isn't buying it. "Did you bring your broomstick with you?" When Dorothy says no, Glinda is matter-of-fact about the alternative: if Dorothy wants to get to Oz, she'll have to walk. Implicit is Glinda's belief that Dorothy herself is more than up to the task.

This film is no typical fairy tale of a damsel in distress. There's no need for a handsome prince to gallop in on a white steed, slay the Wicked Witch, and carry Dorothy safely home. She handles things quite capably on her own, thank you, with a little help from friends she has made along the way. Dorothy will learn more about the extent of her own power shortly, but in the meantime, she's learning not to give it away. This requires pulling back the curtain and seeing things as they really are.

47. Experience + validation = confidence.

The Wizard is nothing if not silver-tongued, but some of what he's saying when he dispenses awards near the end of the film just doesn't make sense. He tells the Tin Man that "hearts will never be practical until they can be made unbreakable," and that "a heart is not judged by how much you love, but by how much you are loved by others." Who says hearts have to be practical? Love is notoriously irrational. And unbreakable? It's vulnerability that is a necessary condition for love, not indestructibility. Otherwise, how could we find out who the other person really is? How could we open ourselves up to their feelings?

As far as hearts being judged by how much we're loved by others, once again the Wizard is wide of the mark. Why do our hearts need to be judged anyway? And who are the "others" doing the judging? If you accept the premise that what matters most is how much we're loved by others, then life turns into one big popularity contest.

Yet despite the fact that some of what the Wizard has to say to the Scarecrow, the Tin Man, and the Cowardly Lion is hot air, Oz's attempts to live up to his promises do have a positive effect. As the Wizard rightly points out, what the Scarecrow, the Tin Man, and the Cowardly Lion lack is confidence. They've earned some of that confidence through experience—by coming to the end of a journey filled with trials and triumphs. Now the Wizard makes his ceremonial contribution.

Psychologist Abraham Maslow famously created a five-tier model of human needs. Fourth in the hierarchy is esteem, which includes both the desire to be respected by others and the need to value oneself. The former is more important for children and adolescents, Maslow said, which would include Dorothy's young companions. This need for validation from other people precedes the achievement of true self-esteem, which explains why that diploma, or medal, or heart-shaped watch makes a difference. Experience plus validation gives the Scarecrow, the Tin Man, and the Cowardly Lion the confidence they need.

48. Once you forgive, then you can forget.

Dorothy is visibly angry to discover the Wizard is a fraud, but she's not going to get stuck in that feeling and become bitter. As she speaks with the man behind the curtain, she finds out more about who he is, and in the process she doesn't just accept his dramatic shortcomings. She goes a step further. Look carefully at her face. Her brief anger gives way to compassion, which allows her to come up with an act of spiritual grace: forgiveness.

Forgiving someone else, or yourself, is challenging. It's far easier to cast blame or play the victim. However, forgiveness is the key to true independence. Once you forgive you're no longer giving away your power, no longer denying your role as director of your own biopic. Interestingly, since Oz mirrors Kansas, when Dorothy forgives the Wizard she is also forgiving Uncle Henry for his inability to stand up to either Miss Gulch or Aunt Em. And by forgiving someone in her own dream, she is also forgiving an aspect of herself— the part of her that would rather follow than lead.

49. Love trumps hate–but not without help from brains, heart, and courage.

Good prevails over evil, at least in *The Wizard of Oz* installment of this ongoing conflict. But don't get complacent. Keep that bucket of water handy. Use your brains to make good choices, your heart to stir compassion, and courage to confront your fears when the outcome looks most uncertain. Answer the call of the Hero's Journey, taking on wicked witches as they appear. This is a struggle for the ages. It always has been, and always will be.

50. Leaving home is the best way to truly appreciate it.

If home is all you know, then like a fish in a pond you're going to take it for granted. To truly appreciate what it means to be home, you have to leave it behind and head off for parts unknown. In addition to returning with lots of new experiences, you'll bring a fresh perspective—and a new appreciation—for what you're returning to. This is what happens in Dorothy's case, although as we'll find out in the last Emerald of Wisdom, additional dimensions to the meaning of *home* will cast her discovery in a new light.

51. Toto means everything.

Spelling *dog* backwards or learning that the Latin word *toto* means "all" may be all you need to confirm the value of bringing a canine into your life. If not, consider that having a dog in your home is one of the best things you can do to keep it safe. Or the medical research showing that dog owners benefit from reduced blood pressure, a higher likelihood of rising up from the couch and going for a walk, and greater overall well-being.

Not only is Toto a steady source of unconditional love for Dorothy (and who doesn't need that?), but at crucial junctures Toto also serves as an agent of change himself. In Kansas he prompts Dorothy to run away, leading to the accident that sends her to Oz. Once there, he's the reason Dorothy stands up to the Cowardly Lion, which not only gives the king of the forest an opportunity to unburden himself of his distorted self-image, but also provides Dorothy with a new ally.

It's Toto who leads the Scarecrow, the Tin Man, and the Cowardly Lion to the witch's castle to free Dorothy from the dungeon. And, of course, it is he who pulls aside the throne room curtain, revealing the game-changing truth about the Great and Powerful Oz. By chasing after a cat just as Dorothy's about to step in the Wizard's balloon, Toto saves his mistress from a long, dangerous flight with a bumbling airman at the controls. What's more, this creates an opening for Glinda to propose a far more satisfying way home, one that allows Dorothy to complete her journey to a fully realized self.

52. It's all about the shoes.

In the end it all comes down to the ultimate accessory. In Baum's *The Wonderful Wizard of Oz* they were silver, but in the MGM film they become the famous Ruby Slippers. In both instances footwear holds the key—the mysterious magic spell that early on compelled Glinda to counsel Dorothy, "Keep tight inside of them. Their magic must be very powerful." Now that Dorothy has attained the wisdom she came for, the slippers stand ready to do their part.

EMERALD OF WISDOM
8

**You've got the power,
and you've had it all along.**

As a cheery throng of Emerald City residents turns out to wish their departing leader farewell, Toto leaps out of the gondola of the Wizard's balloon to chase a cat in the crowd. When Dorothy goes after her dog, the Wizard lifts off without them, unable to control his own aircraft. Dorothy's ride home is floating away and it won't be back.

While her friends try unsuccessfully to console her, the same glowing pink bubble that marked Dorothy's arrival in Oz approaches, and Glinda steps out. This time the kindly Witch of the North presents Dorothy with a dramatic revelation: "You don't need to be helped any longer. You've always had the power to go back to Kansas." The Scarecrow, ever

Dorothy's defender, asks, "Then why didn't you tell her before?" Glinda replies, "Because she wouldn't have believed me. She had to learn it for herself." We're nearing the film's grand finale. For Dorothy the shift within herself is nearly complete. All she needs is one last nudge, and Glinda is there to provide it.

The lesson that you have the power to realize your own heart's desire and you've had it all along cannot be taught. As Glinda points out, you have to learn it for yourself. Dorothy has followed the trail of Emeralds of Wisdom like bread crumbs. She has listened to her longing, anchored herself in awareness of this moment, celebrated herself and the Munchkins for showing up, greeted everyone with loving-kindness, overcome the self-delusions embodied by her friends, faced her fears, and pulled back the curtain to see things as they are. Now she discovers that she possesses the power to achieve her heart's desire: to return home. She has accumulated this wisdom on her Hero's Journey, while liberating the Munchkin and Winkie people from the two most powerful witches in the Land of Oz. She has made allies along the Yellow Brick Road, and exposed the Great and Powerful Oz as a charlatan. Now Dorothy stands on the brink of a quantum leap into adulthood. She's ready to take responsibility for her own life.

In the everyday world we celebrate such momentous occasions in various ways, but here in Emerald City, Glinda is ordained by virtue of her magic to initiate Dorothy into full awareness of her own powers. The young woman's three closest friends are in attendance, along with the thousands of green-clad citizens who gathered in the city square to bid farewell to the Wizard, but now bear silent witness to Dorothy's rite of passage. As Glinda comes to Dorothy's aid once again, the Witch of the North makes it clear that this will be the last time.

Physically, Dorothy hasn't changed since she stepped out of her airlifted farmhouse, at least not perceptibly. Her body may be a little stronger from all that walking, but the principal transformations have come from within. Having metabolized her experiences in Oz, Dorothy is now ready to cross a sacred threshold. One last element remains before Dorothy's passage is secured, and Glinda provides it: awareness. Without it, the magic in the Ruby Slippers is useless, as inert as Excalibur embedded in its scabbard of stone. But once Dorothy becomes aware of their potential, these slippers can transport her across worlds, from Oz to Kansas, with three clicks of their heels and the repetition of a simple phrase.

This is the moment in *The Wizard of Oz* that speaks most directly to me. This lesson is the one I needed to live by writing this book. I felt the powerlessness of childhood keenly. With the tangled logic of a child, I correlated physical strength directly with power; since I lacked the one, it made sense that I should lack the other. *The Wizard of Oz* challenges this assumption, opening up the possibility that power is held not just by adults; it is not just something calibrated by body size and muscle mass. Nor is it a matter of controlling others.

Like the magic in the Ruby Slippers, power is activated by both experience and awareness, and supported by the very same qualities that Dorothy personifies on her journey along the Yellow Brick Road. Yes, we do have the power to fulfill our heart's desire, and we possessed it all along. It's a lesson I'm still learning, one I need to remind myself of every day, but I know that in a film that loves exposing illusions, we've finally peeled away that last curtain and arrived at the truth.

But wait! There's more! Dorothy is still in Oz, and one final Emerald awaits discovery. As it becomes clear how much depends on Dorothy's new insight, the Tin Man comes right out and asks for clarification. "What have you learned, Dorothy?" To which she replies: "That if I ever go looking for my heart's desire again, I won't look any further than my own backyard; because if it isn't there, I never really lost it to begin with. Is that right?" Glinda nods in affirmation: "That's all it is."

So now we have an explanation for *where* Dorothy's insight is located. But what about the insight itself? As if to help straighten out its convoluted message, Glinda tells Dorothy that the last step to awaken the magic power of the Ruby Slippers requires Dorothy to think to herself: "There's no place like home, there's no place like home, there's no place like home. . . ."

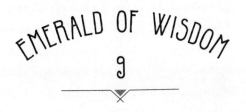

EMERALD OF WISDOM

9

There's no place like home.

This time the message is clear and, on the face of it, indisputable. But how satisfying is it as the conclusion to this remarkable film? Over the years, critics have both gushed over and gored many aspects of *The Wizard of Oz*, but its ending in particular has come under heavy attack. A cop-out in an otherwise groundbreaking film, a wobbly finale tacked on to satisfy Hollywood's requirement for a happy ending: this is how the naysaying arguments go.

At first glance, it's difficult to see why Dorothy would pass up life in Technicolor Oz for a return to sepia-toned Kansas, yet I don't question the rightness of the ending. Why? Because it has passed the ultimate litmus test: eight decades after this film first hit theaters, we're still talking about it. Since that's just not possible for a movie with a disappointing ending, let's take a closer look at how the conclusion succeeds in its all-important mission, despite making an awkward first impression.

I recognize the dissonance between "there's no place like home" and Dorothy's desire to travel over the rainbow. The tension between Dorothy's fear of losing Aunt Em and Dorothy's desire to make a life of her own still needs to be resolved. For answers we turn back to the beginning of the film, to the moment that set everything in motion. If desire is the engine of the universe, as the mystical sages of Kabbalah believe, then Dorothy's longing creates the forward thrust for *The Wizard of Oz*. What exactly does she yearn for? Well, it changes, just as Dorothy does. At first she longs for a place far from the life she's leading. Yet when Dorothy's dream really *does* come true, she realizes that it's not the idyll she imagined. Aided by Emeralds of Wisdom, Dorothy succeeds in melting her nemesis, but not with the effortless ease of sucking a lemon drop. Much is demanded of Dorothy in Oz, so much, in fact, that during her travels there, she grows up.

As the film wraps up back in Kansas, Dorothy takes stock. Some of what's important to her hasn't changed from that moment when she stepped into the barnyard and began to sing. It's what matters most to any child and what Aunt Em represents: safety and love. When Almira Gulch rides off with Toto in her basket, that sense of security has been violated, and Aunt Em's and Uncle Henry's affection called into question. At the end of the film, however, these needs still matter to Dorothy, but not in the way they do to a child; her journey through Oz has brought her hard-won wisdom and maturity, and with it a shift in perspective.

Now she knows that wickedness is a feature of every landscape, just as goodness is. This means that from time to time bad things are going to happen, through no fault of Aunt Em and Uncle Henry. It's true that they didn't do a great job of protecting Toto, although we get the distinct impression that they would have made any sacrifice to protect Dorothy herself. However, as caregivers they're flawed, just like the rest of us, which means that the safety they can provide for Dorothy and Toto is imperfect, too.

So is their love. On the action-packed day of the cyclone, Dorothy's aunt and uncle are impatient, making it clear to Dorothy that she's a pest. Her sense of home under siege, Dorothy runs away, but even while she's still in Kansas she realizes Aunt Em loves her and will miss her terribly. In Oz, Dorothy becomes more and more aware of the depths of her own love for Aunt Em. There's nothing like the clarity provided by a close brush with death.

After her extended adventures in Oz, Dorothy also comes to appreciate just how much safety her aunt and uncle do provide, even if that umbrella doesn't cover Toto. In Oz, Dorothy begins to set aside her childish dreams of *perfect* safety and *perfect* love. She takes the first steps in a process that lasts a lifetime, where dreams of perfection give way to gratitude for *good-enough* protection and *good-enough* love. In the world as it is, these possess great value and are worth striving to return to. Home is coming to mean something new to Dorothy, something precious. For all its flaws, there is no place like it.

There is yet another way to make sense of the film's conclusion, which goes like this. When Dorothy realizes there's no place like home, she's not just referring to the farmhouse where she lives with Aunt Em and Uncle Henry. Yes, as their child she misses them; she's only twelve years old, after all. But with wisdom newly accumulated in Oz, Dorothy is pointing to something beyond a construct of wood and plaster, to a space she has come to locate within herself. Here she has internalized the power she once deferred to others, which in itself is a tremendous accomplishment. Yet the reaches of this inner landscape extend far beyond the boundaries of psychology.

Dorothy has discovered a conduit to the vast realm of the collective unconscious. The home to which she's referring is less a physical place than it is a feeling, and less a feeling than it is a state of being. In fact, it is the ground state of *all* being. This is the spiritual infinitude from which each of us rises up briefly in this lifetime, like a wave on the ocean, individual yet wholly connected, before falling back to merge with the endless depths from which we came. Dorothy's true home (and yours and mine) is the boundless wellspring of creation, the divine force that animates every religion and imbues every aspect of the universe with energy.

Home. Say it slowly. The letter *h* contributes what's known as a voiceless sound. Let that go, and what's left vibrates from your vocal cords. In the ancient Hindu wisdom tradition all of creation sprang from this word-sound, *Om.* It's the original sound, within which everything is contained. As one of the great Vedic texts puts it, "Whosoever knows this one syllable obtains all that he desires." *Om* is the primordial mother. *Om* is the home we all carry within us.

Thich Nhat Hanh likes to bring to mind a little poem many times during the day—when he eats, when he washes the dishes, and when he meditates:

> *I have arrived, I am home,*
> *In the here and in the now.*
> *I am solid, I am free,*
> *In the ultimate I dwell.*

Every household chore, every bite, every breath, reminds this Zen monk that he is home.

This is the final lesson Dorothy brings back from her travels through Oz. This is the Golden Fleece of her mythological Hero's Journey, the priceless treasure at the end of the successful quest. It is the emerald brought up from the deepest mine shaft, truth at its most hard-won and profound. The longing that launched Dorothy on her journey—and inspires us to set out on our own—has finally found both its source and its fulfillment. Home is where you are right now. You and I are home in this moment . . . and in this one . . . and in this one, too. We are home in each breath. We are home in the spacious awareness that lies within us and also extends infinitely far beyond us to include all of existence in its embrace. We are home because, like Dorothy, we never left; we just needed to become aware of this in order to return.

PART THREE

Putting the Emeralds to Work

WORKING TOGETHER, THE Emeralds of Wisdom perform a special function above and beyond their appearance in a larger list of insights. Arranged in linear progression as if along Dorothy's path, they can also combine to serve as an astonishingly effective tool whenever life requires us to embark on our own Hero's Journey. Here's how it works.

Imagine an old-fashioned overhead projector. On the brightly lit glass surface you've placed a transparency that is now being cast into bright relief on the wall opposite you. This is a two-dimensional rendering of whatever obstacle may be currently facing you, a visual landscape in which your mission is to get from *A* to *Z*. It might involve other people: an argument with your partner; a problem at work with your boss; a rift that needs to be healed with parents, or siblings, or an old friend. Or, it might only concern you: feelings of loneliness; low self-worth; lack of self-control around food, or alcohol, or drugs. Whatever fraught landscape you're facing, its image is now being projected onto the wall before you.

Now take another transparency and set it on top of the acetate already in your projector. This new transparency is the Oz Overlay, which indicates the location of each Emerald of Wisdom. As the projector merges the two sets of images into one, you will see the Emeralds now are arranged like way stations marking nine crucial moments during Dorothy's progress through Oz. Now, keeping the landscape of your particular problem in the background, run through the nine Emeralds much the way Dorothy did in her dream of Oz.

If this metaphor feels unwieldy, consider a more direct approach: look at your particular issue and ask yourself, What would Dorothy do? Well, she'd do what she did in Oz, which worked spectacularly well. Now you can do the same. Whenever you're faced with a problem that seems insurmountable, run through the nine Emeralds of Wisdom in order, one after the other.

By the way, this practice needn't take long. You can pause for just a few seconds at each Emerald, especially once you become familiar with the process. For your convenience, here they are, all in one place.

THE NINE EMERALDS

1. **Listen to your longing (page 26).** What do you yearn for in this situation? Is it possible? Is it helpful? This is the moment to remember your deeper longing for connection—to become aware that you are immersed in an ocean of spiritual energy that contains everyone and everything. Is your lesser longing going to move you toward that goal?

2. **See the world as if for the first time (page 42).** What preconceptions can you set aside as you consider the issue you may be facing? How can you view it with fresh eyes, as if for the first time?

Pausing at this way station, remind yourself just how special each experience is in a lifetime that's racing by with stunning speed, and sit quietly in this moment right now.

3. **Celebrate yourself—and others—for showing up (page 49).** The world you're looking out on is miraculous, and it's a reflection of you. Remember to celebrate yourself for your willingness to participate. It's wonderful that you've chosen to show up!

4. **Choose compassion (page 59).** Put yourself in the other person's shoes. Assume that they have the same basic needs and desires you do, and a question naturally arises: How can I help? Now that you've opened the floodgates of compassion, direct it to yourself as well.

5. **You already possess what you desire most (page 68).** If you didn't already have it, you wouldn't know to long for it. Anything else that you're chasing is just illusion. Whatever qualities you admire most in other people are already central to who you are.

6. **Face what you fear (page 85).** It's the only way to make it smaller. If it turns out to be nothing but

shadows, move on. If the threat is real, greet it with compassion. It may prove surprisingly easy to melt.

7. **Pull back the curtain and see things as they really are (page 100).** When you were a child, you relied on your parents to chart your course. But by the time you're old enough to read these words, the terms of that arrangement are already changing. You're stepping into the leadership role in your life, and that's as it should be. No worries, you've got this. If you have any lingering doubts, the next Emerald will dispel them.

8. **You've got the power, and you've had it all along (page 110).** As long as you don't give it away before you realize how valuable it is (hang on to those Ruby Slippers!), you can settle into your birthright as conductor of the orchestra of your life. (The musicians, like Dorothy's friends in her dream, are all you!)

9. **There's no place like home (page 115).** The place where you hang your hat is special, if only because you are there. Then there's the other home, too, the one inside you. This in turn opens up into the home we all share, the spiritual source of all things, from which we arise to experience this lifetime, and to which we will all return.

I like to use the Emeralds to run through a quick "What would Dorothy do?" (WWDD) exercise in my mind before going into an important meeting, or as I prepare to resolve a difference with my wife or with someone else in my life. In the heat of the moment, it's not always possible to pause long enough to consider nine insights; it's often all I can do to take a few deep breaths. But running through the Emeralds of Wisdom quickly in your mind (try to keep them in order) turns out to be great preparation for successfully overcoming obstacles.

In my case, as a child I loved to perform onstage, yet as an adult I developed a fear of public speaking. As an editor it's important to be able to present your books to a room full of marketing people, for instance, or at a sales conference, which could include an audience of one hundred or more. Eventually I became pretty good at it, and I can see now that the techniques I relied on were a fledgling version of the nine Emeralds. Today I flash through them in my mind just before stepping up to the microphone. It goes something like this:

I long to both entertain and edify my audience, so that when the evening is over, they leave feeling uplifted and a bit more capable of addressing whatever obstacles to happiness they're facing.

Beginner's Mind is a tool I can use to experience this moment as if for the first time. Let me slow things down so I can appreciate their beauty and fully savor every aspect of inhabiting this space, right here and right now.

How lucky I am to be me! This is my moment, just as it is for everyone else in this room, and I'm going to seize it joyfully!

In my compassion I can imagine walking a mile in the shoes of the people gathered here; I have a heartfelt desire to improve their lives, if only for a few moments. I also extend this compassion to myself.

What do I desire most in this situation? It's courage. That self-doubt is just an illusion. I've got this!

I'm facing my fear that I'll seize up and be incapable of saying a word, that I'll be humiliated. Okay, take a deep breath or two. Reach for that compassion again, and apply it to yourself. Remember that tonight you're a vehicle for transmitting information to the people gathered here. Whatever happens, you'll be the better for it, and so will they.

I'm not giving my power away. This moment is mine. Once I've put this oxygen mask on, I can reach out to put it on whoever needs help nearby, but it begins right here with me.

To be powerful in this moment is my birthright. I've got the power and I've had it all along. As Jimi Hendrix put it, "I'm the one that's got to die when it's time for me to die, so let me live my life the way I want to." What better time than now?

Home is right here inside me, just as it is for everyone in this room. We're connected. We're all sharing this moment, right now. Let's enjoy it. A rising tide lifts all boats, and as I look out at the audience I realize that I am that tide. We all are.

A Reverie of Oz

Do you ever wonder what would have happened to Dorothy if *The Wizard of Oz* had followed her story a little longer? How did her experiences in Oz change her, and what effect would they have had on the rest of her life? We see signs of a shift in the film's final scene, when Dorothy recuperates in bed while being fussed over by family and friends, each of whom echoes a character in her dream. She seems calmer, more assertive, and more confident than she did earlier in Kansas. But what will take place in a few days, after the novelty of her near-death experience wears off, along with all that solicitous attention she's getting? And what happened to the challenges Dorothy faced before the cyclone hit?

Assuming Miss Gulch survived the storm (might Dorothy's dream have been a premonition of Almira's death?), she might choose to abandon her vengeful pursuit of Toto. But if she persists in her efforts to kill the dog of a girl who nearly died in a twister, Almira is going to run into a whirlwind of opposition. Local sympathies will run heavily in favor of Dorothy, and keeping the next election in mind, the sheriff will see the wisdom in sorting things out accordingly, even if that means a certain terrier spends more time on the leash.

In my imaginings the wisdom acquired in Dorothy's dream will continue to shape her life. Now that she has found a locus of power both within and larger than herself, Dorothy continues to evolve. Her schoolbooks provide transport to another world far from the farm where Aunt Em and Uncle Henry raised her. She applies herself to her studies with the single-minded focus of someone who has survived a near-death experience, and she leverages that extraordinary singing voice to get a scholarship.

Dorothy chooses a college close enough to home so she can visit her aunt and uncle regularly, yet far enough so she can enjoy her independence. Having awakened to her inner landscape, Dorothy takes up a spiritual practice. She might choose to follow in her aunt's footsteps and become a regular at church, or she might meditate, explore Buddhism, or find her own way to nourish the connection to the home within that she discovered in Oz.

May similar good things come true for you, dear reader, in whatever way best satisfies your longings. Thank you for joining me on the journey of these pages. Wherever you may be on your path through life, may the wisdom in the Emeralds of Oz deepen and enrich your experience, and help us all to make this world a better place.

Appendix:

A BRIEF BOOK AND FILM HISTORY

IN ORDER TO become more knowledgeable about *The Wizard of Oz* as I prepared to write this book, I did a lot of reading about Frank Baum, his book, and the MGM film based on it—including some fascinating information on how the film was made. If finding out how sausage is made can turn carnivores into vegetarians, you would think dissecting this film for its cinematic magic would have an equally off-putting effect, but once again ordinary rules don't apply to *The Wizard of Oz*.

While writing this book I watched the movie countless times, poring over it frame by frame in search of hidden meanings and lessons. Astonishingly, this did nothing to dampen the affection I've felt for the film since I was a child. In fact, I take more pleasure watching *The Wizard of Oz* now than ever before. It is in this spirit of happy bafflement and admiration that I offer the following brief compendium of bits and pieces of information about the book and the movie that I collected along my way.

As the nineteenth century began to turn the page into the twentieth, Frank Baum doused the kerosene lantern on his desk in Chicago's Humboldt Park. After having tried his hand at numerous professions, from acting to publishing a trade journal about poultry, from selling lubricating oil to working as a buyer for a department store, Baum had just put the finishing touches on his latest venture: a children's book. It was October 9, 1899, and Frank Baum sensed that with *The Wonderful Wizard of Oz* he'd accomplished something special.

He would never know how fervently the world would come to agree with him, although the book did become a best seller in the United States with the help of imaginative illustrations from Baum's collaborator, William Wallace Denslow. In 1902 a stage musical extravaganza based on the book was also a commercial success. The money generated by book and ticket sales was a godsend to Baum, whose many enthusiasms left his personal finances cycling between boom and bust.

After the success of *The Wonderful Wizard of Oz*, Baum wrote several forgettable unrelated books before clamoring readers and an empty purse prompted him to write *The Marvelous Land of Oz*, the first of thirteen sequels to his magnum opus. A dispute over royalties had led to a rupture with Denslow, yet even without his illustrations the new Oz books became hugely popular. After Baum died in 1919, his publishers arranged for several writers to continue the series. Eventually its total number would reach forty.

The MGM film we know and love was not the first movie based on Baum's *The Wonderful Wizard of Oz*. Much like the theatrical production in 1902, the 1910 Selig Polyscope film and the later 1925 Chadwick Productions film took great liberties with the book that inspired it. In the stage musical Toto is replaced by Imogene, a pet cow, for instance, and in the Chadwick film Dorothy, a flapper from Kansas deposited on Aunt Em and Uncle Henry's doorstep as a baby, travels to Oz to reclaim her rightful throne. Despite the presence of Oliver Hardy—who would later famously team up with Stan Laurel—as the Tin Woodman, the Chadwick picture tanked. In any event, it would soon have been relegated to oblivion by a transformative breakthrough in cinematic technology: sound.

Nearly twenty years after the death of L. Frank Baum, his oldest son, Frank J. Baum, made the rounds in Hollywood to sell the film rights. He struck a deal with Samuel Goldwyn, the irascible movie mogul who had already parted ways with the company that bore his name, Metro-Goldwyn-Mayer. Four years later, when Sam Goldwyn decided to auction *The Wonderful Wizard of Oz*, two studios got into a bidding war. One was Goldwyn's former company, MGM, and the other was Twentieth Century Fox, which was looking for a new vehicle for the studio's child star, Shirley Temple. What a different film that would have been!

MGM, however, came away with the prize and chose Judy Garland, a child actress successfully paired with Mickey Rooney in three movies, to play the lead. Goldwyn nearly doubled his original investment with a sale price of $75,000 (about $1.3 million today). That figure would eventually be described by the film's producer as one of the biggest bargains of all time— right alongside the Louisiana Purchase—but that moment lay far in the future.

MGM, which cranked out dozens of films each year, anointed *The Wizard of Oz* one of its prestige releases. Well financed though it was, the movie still had great difficulty coming into the world. More than a dozen screenwriters worked on *The Wizard of Oz* in an often-overlapping effort that its producer, Mervyn LeRoy, described as "a giant headache." As a result, the plot became almost laughably ornate. In one of screenwriter Noel Langley's versions, for instance, Dorothy gets romantically involved with Hickory, Miss Gulch is Dorothy's schoolteacher, Aunt Em is cruel, and when the story shifts to Oz, Uncle Henry becomes Bulbo, the son of the Wicked Witch of the West. Ultimately, most problems with the script were resolved by moving back in the direction of Frank Baum's book.

On the all-important musical side of the production, the studio brought in composer Harold Arlen, who had written the music for a number of hit songs, including "Let's Fall in Love" and "Stormy Weather." He was teamed up with lyricist Edgar "Yip" Harburg, who had written the words to hits like "Brother, Can You Spare a Dime?," "April in Paris," and "It's Only a Paper Moon." Arlen and Harburg had less than four months to come up with the complete musical score for this monumental project. Unlike the screenwriters, they were working without benefit of a blueprint equivalent to Baum's book. They were further challenged by their desire to do something altogether new. At the time, musicals paused their narrative completely to allow actors and actresses to break into song and dance, but Arlen and Harburg wanted each song to work as an integral part of the story.

Like the music and the screenwriting, the filming of *The Wizard of Oz* also struggled under the burden of ambition. Heavily made-up and elaborately costumed actors sweltered under the countless bright lights required to shoot in Technicolor, a recent breakthrough in film technology. Bert Lahr, wrapped in two lion skins filled out with padding, suffered more than most. Shortly after shooting began, Buddy Ebsen, playing the Tin Man, was rushed to the hospital in critical condition after inhaling his aluminum powder makeup, to be replaced by Jack Haley. Margaret Hamilton, whose brilliant embodiment of the Wicked Witch of the West would terrify generations of viewers, burned the skin off her hand during the Munchkinland scenes. While she spent nearly six weeks recovering in the hospital, her stand-in, Betty Danko, was seriously injured during the very same scenes when her smoking broomstick exploded.

After overcoming all these obstacles and more, on August 25, 1939, MGM released *The Wizard of Oz*, based on Frank Baum's novel, starring Frank Morgan as the Wizard, Ray Bolger as the Scarecrow, Jack Haley as the Tin Man, Bert Lahr as the Cowardly Lion, Margaret Hamilton as the Wicked Witch of the West, and of course Judy Garland as Dorothy. Most reviews were favorable, but the film's launch was marred by unfortunate timing. *The Wizard of Oz* was released in a year that is widely considered the best ever for film, alongside such future classics as *Mr. Smith Goes to Washington*, *Stagecoach*, *Only Angels Have Wings*, *The Hunchback of Notre Dame*, *Wuthering Heights*, *Of Mice and Men*, and *Goodbye, Mr. Chips*. It was also the year of *Gone With the Wind*, which swept the Academy Awards, leaving *The Wizard of Oz* to garner only two competitive Oscars—Best Musical Adaptation, and Best Song for "Somewhere Over the Rainbow." (Judy Garland received a special award for outstanding performance as a screen juvenile.) Box office sales for *The Wizard of Oz* were respectable, but decades would go by before the studio turned a profit.

On November 3, 1956, more than seventeen years after its initial release, *The Wizard of Oz* stepped into its starring role in American culture. This was the day CBS first aired the film on television. Aired again as a Christmas special three years later, in 1959, *The Wizard of Oz* was so well received that it became an annual television staple for the next forty years! Several years after that tradition began, my family joined the swelling tide of Americans who made viewing it a not-to-be-missed event. In 1999, the new owner of *The Wizard of Oz*, Warner Bros. Television, a division of Turner Entertainment, began showing the movie several times each year.

Today *The Wizard of Oz* is celebrated all over the world. Translated into forty languages, it is every bit as beloved in Japan, India, and Australia as it is in the United States. The universal themes in L. Frank Baum's first truly American fairy tale have touched the hearts and fired the imaginations of viewers across both space and time, with no end in sight.

Watching a film, like attending a play or reading a novel, requires something from the viewer: the willing suspension of disbelief. The creators of the narrative must do their part as well, providing a story that pulls the reader in from the beginning and doesn't let go until the final frame. *The Wizard of Oz* acquits its end of this bargain beautifully. When it's over, I feel like I've just seen a performance by a world-class magician. Although I know I should just go home happy, I can't help but wonder how it was done. Where did that rabbit come from? How did the stoic assistant survive being sawed in half?

A good magician never reveals the secrets behind

those tricks, but it's more difficult to be discreet about the making of a film. Everyone involved has a story to tell, and over the years it's likely to come out, especially once it becomes clear that this particular film is one for the ages. Here are some tidbits about the making of the movie that may surprise and entertain you.

In 1922, Judy Garland was born Frances Ethel Gumm to vaudeville parents, and by age two and a half Judy's ambitious mother had pushed her into a stage debut, singing with her older sisters, Mary Jane and Dorothy. By the time Frances was six, she had become a full-fledged member of the Gumm Sisters song-and-dance act, which would become the Garland Sisters in late 1934. The following year the newly renamed Judy Garland signed a contract with MGM to become part of its stable of actors and actresses. Petite at what would be her full adult height of four foot eleven, Garland was considered by the studio to be overweight and unattractive in an era that prized glamor. However, Arthur Freed, the assistant producer on *The Wizard of Oz*, saw it as the perfect vehicle for Garland's singing and acting talents.

There's a blooper in the first Kansas part of the film, when Aunt Em comes outside with fresh-baked crullers.

"Here, here," she says, "what's all this jabber-wapping when there's work to be done!" Hickory tries to explain, "Well, Dorothy was walking along—" but Aunt Em interrupts him. *"I saw you tinkering with that contraption, Hickory!* Now you and Hunk get back to that wagon." What contraption is she talking about? It turns out that in an earlier version of the movie Hickory used an old boiler, wires, tubes, and a motor to create a gizmo capable of countering the effect of windstorms. On the day of the cyclone he used it, but the scene ended up on the cutting room floor; all that remains is Aunt Em's now-mystifying comment.

The idea for the visually striking moment when sepia-toned Kansas gives way to Technicolor Oz was borrowed from W. W. Denslow, Baum's illustrator, who used this same approach in his artwork for *The Wonderful Wizard of Oz*.

Actor W. C. Fields was considered first in line for the role of Professor Marvel and the Wizard. However, after contract negotiations broke down MGM turned to Frank Morgan. Morgan, who died in 1949, was the one major cast member who would not live to see *The Wizard of Oz* take its place at the pinnacle of the American film pantheon.

Did you know that the song "Over the Rainbow" nearly didn't make it into *The Wizard of Oz*? When a gathering of producers at MGM watched a preview of the movie, they agreed that Judy Garland's signature song didn't work. As a result Louis B. Mayer, who ruled the roost at MGM, cut the song for the second preview. Later, after several key executives argued to keep "Over the Rainbow," the song went back in. Today it's impossible to imagine the film without it. When my children were little, this was the lullaby that I crooned to them every night at bedtime.

Although Victor Fleming is credited as the director of *The Wizard of Oz*, he did not actually complete the film. MGM, which employed Fleming, lent him out to David O. Selznick in order to direct MGM's other big film that year, *Gone With the Wind*. The rest of the movie, including the parts set in Kansas, were directed by King Vidor, who was not credited for his contribution.

A persistent rumor about *The Wizard of Oz* links it to Pink Floyd's *Dark Side of the Moon*. The band denies that the album was written to play over the first forty-three minutes of the movie, but if you start the CD at precisely the moment the MGM lion completes its third roar you can listen yourself and arrive at your own conclusion. There are certainly some moments of astonishing synchronicity in this mash-up of two classics.

Bill Gates may have dropped out of college, but L. Frank Baum never even earned a high school diploma. At age twelve Baum went to Peekskill Military Academy for two years, but he disliked the strict discipline there and did not return. Instead, he stayed home with his parents near Syracuse, New York, and continued his education with private tutors.

With the exception of the brief shot of clouds behind the film's main titles, *The Wizard of Oz* was filmed entirely indoors, on MGM's many soundstages.

During a preview of *The Wizard of Oz*, when it was being tested on audiences before being released to movie theaters, some small children were so terrified by Margaret Hamilton's portrayal of Miss Gulch and the Wicked Witch of the West that they had to leave the theater. As a result, the film went back to editing, and Hamilton's scenes were trimmed in order to make them less frightening. One casualty, if you can call it that, was a threat by the Wicked Witch of the West to cut off Dorothy's feet in order to lay claim to the Ruby Slippers.

If you haven't watched the 1975 episode of *Mister Rogers' Neighborhood* where he interviews Margaret Hamilton, I recommend it. Their conversation about make-believe finally allowed me to put the terrors of the cackling Wicked Witch behind me, once and for all.

For the scenes shot in Munchkinland, MGM hired the services of 124 "Singer Midgets," who would all live together in the Culver City Hotel during filming. Despite being notably short herself, sixteen-year-old Judy Garland towered over the adult men and women that the makeup department would laboriously transform into Munchkins.

Women play an unusually important role in *The Wizard of Oz*, given the era when the film was made. It's no coincidence that Frank Baum's mother-in-law, Matilda Gage, was a prominent figure in the suffragette movement, alongside Susan B. Anthony and Elizabeth Cady Stanton. Like the women who inspired Baum's fictional heroine, Dorothy also generated controversy. She was so capable and confident that some considered her subversive: both the Chicago and

Detroit public libraries banned *The Wonderful Wizard of Oz* in 1928 and 1957, respectively.

Oz itself is a matriarchy, in which power is concentrated in the hands of good and wicked witches. At first the Wizard of Oz looks to be the one exception, but his greatness turns out to be nothing more than smoke, fire, and inflated accounts of his own importance. The only man with any power in Oz turns out to be a humbug.

It's fortunate for all of us that in the bidding for film rights to *The Wizard of Oz*, MGM prevailed, and not just because of Judy Garland. MGM, known as "the Tiffany of the business," had the ambition, the deep pockets, and the vast on-site arts and crafts department needed to create all the special effects, costumes, and scenery that contribute to the film's on-screen magic. (Did you know that the field of poppies required wiring an acre of artificial poppies by hand?) And, of course, the studio hired top-drawer producers, directors, screenwriters, songwriters, lyricists, cinematographers, and actors as well.

More than twenty years after the film was released Judy Garland described some of the hardships she endured while playing Dorothy Gale. "I was fat, had crooked teeth, straight and black hair, and the wrong kind of nose. So they made me wear a corset and a wig, capped my teeth, and put horrible things in my nose to turn it up like Shirley's [Shirley Temple's]." Although the wig was eventually scrapped, Judy Garland would drop twelve pounds thanks to a strictly enforced diet and an exercise regimen created by Barbara "Bobbie" Koshay, an Olympic swimmer who also served as Garland's camera double in the film. It was Koshay who actually tumbled into the pig-pen, who was carried off by the Winged Monkeys, and who opened the door to the farmhouse just before Garland stepped out onto the Munchkinland plaza.

What do Ben Hecht, Conrad Richter, James Hilton, Dorothy Parker, Lillian Hellman, Robert Benchley, Dashiell Hammett, S. J. Perelman, F. Scott Fitzgerald, John O'Hara, and William Faulkner have in common? At one time or another they were all members of the huge stable of talented writers on the MGM payroll and they *did not* work on *The Wizard of Oz*.

Do you know which actor in *The Wizard of Oz* was the highest paid? Ray Bolger and Jack Haley would have shared that distinction, since both received $3,000 per week for their contributions. However, Haley returned $1,000 per week so he could take time off to record his radio show, so Bolger emerged with the honor. Judy Garland's salary was $750 for every week she was on the picture. The lowest paid regularly appearing actress? Toto (and her handler/owner, Carl Spitz) earned $125 per week. Yep, in real life Toto was a female cairn terrier named Terry!

How prolific was L. Frank Baum, author of *The Wonderful Wizard of Oz*? He wrote fifty-five novels, including fourteen set in Oz, more than eighty short stories, more than two hundred poems, and numerous scripts for the stage.

A second significant blooper takes place after Dorothy and her companions take their leave of the Wizard and set off through the Haunted Forest to find the castle of the Wicked Witch of the West. After watching them through her crystal ball, the witch commands Nikko, leader of the Winged Monkeys, to take his army and bring back the girl and her dog. "They'll give you no trouble, I promise you that. I've sent a little insect on ahead to take the fight out of them!" Huh?

It turns out that at one point the movie contained an elaborate, jazzy song-and-dance number in which a Jitter Bug casts a spell on Dorothy and her friends, forcing them to dance frenetically until they're too exhausted to offer the Winged Monkeys any resistance. The Jitter Bug scene cost $80,000 to produce, but it didn't survive the first preview (yes, it was the same screening that almost led to clipping out "Over the Rainbow").

The Wizard of Oz was anointed an important film right from the beginning. In 1939, the year that *The Wizard of Oz* was released, MGM cranked out an astonishing forty-one films! Small movies cost between $250,000 and $500,000 to produce and were completed in less than a month; big ones were slated for eight weeks. Earmarked from the first as a major release, *The Wizard of Oz* was anticipated to cost a little over $2 million. It would end up taking twenty-two weeks to produce, coming in nearly $800,000 over budget.

There are various explanations for the source of the name "Oz," including several given by Frank Baum himself, although the author was known to bend the truth in service of a good story. Among the two most enduring theories are: Baum took the name from one of his file cabinets, labeled "*O–Z*"; *Oz* stands for "ounce," in this case an ounce of gold or silver, reflecting Baum's enthusiasm for moving the nation away from the gold standard to include silver, freeing up money in a tight economy.

Judy Garland got an uncontrollable fit of the giggles while filming the scene when the Cowardly Lion jumps out of the forest to threaten the Scarecrow, the Tin Man, Dorothy, and Toto. When, after countless takes, Garland still couldn't keep from laughing at Bert Lahr's antics, Victor Fleming, the film's no-nonsense director, slapped Judy and told her to go back to her dressing room. When she returned the scene was shot without a hitch. Despite Fleming's behavior, Garland developed a crush on the handsome director. The incident reflects how different times were then, not just with regard to corporal punishment but also with the nearly unlimited power held by directors in a Hollywood studio system where actors were salaried employees.

Margaret Hamilton, who played the Wicked Witch of the West, didn't suffer as much from her costume as some of the other principals, but she didn't get off lightly, either. Her green makeup smeared easily, so once she was in costume it was almost impossible for her to eat, or even go to the bathroom. Also, after several weeks of wearing the makeup her skin took on a sickly green color. "It must have been months before my face was really normal again," she recalled.

At one point the film explained why the Winged Monkeys served the Wicked Witch of the West, but a scene in the witch's tower room where she says "Bring me my wishing cap. I'll call the Winged Monkeys to fetch me those slippers" was cut from the script. In the film there is still a vestigial reference to this bit of background; in the witch's castle we catch a brief glimpse of the Golden Cap.

Margaret Hamilton was quite comfortable with her own lack of physical beauty. When she was a child her father wanted to have her nose altered by a plastic surgeon, but she refused. "It was mine, and I wanted to keep it."

Many shots of Dorothy Gale where her face is not visible were actually played by her double, Bobbie Koshay. This was a purely pragmatic decision, as described by Oz experts Jay Scarfone and William Stillman, authors of five first-rate books on the film. "Because she was a juvenile, Garland's on-set time was rigidly restricted to accommodate four hours of work, three hours of school, and one hour of recreation, as required by California law."

Toto joined the roster of injured Oz actors when one of the Winkies accidentally stepped on her foot and broke it. Toto/Terry was also so unhappy with the powerful wind machines that blew across the Kansas set that she hid behind the legs of her human costars to avoid the fierce gusts. Terry appeared in at least fifteen films, and in 2011 a permanent memorial for her was dedicated at the Hollywood Forever Cemetery in Los Angeles.

In a strange bit of coincidence (or was it something more?), when MGM's wardrobe department went looking for a slightly seedy Prince Albert coat for Professor Marvel to wear, they found just the right item in a used clothing store. One day, actor Frank Morgan felt something in the jacket, and when he turned its pocket inside out he found the name L. FRANK BAUM stitched into it. A little research confirmed that indeed the coat had once belonged to the creator of Oz. After the film finished shooting, it was returned to his widow, Maud. This story is true, but it sounds like something straight out of *The Twilight Zone*!

The film's famous Ruby Slippers replaced Frank Baum's original silver slippers because red looked so much more dramatic in Technicolor. Four pairs of Ruby Slippers were created by MGM's chief costume designer in 1938, Gilbert Adrian, made from white pumps covered with red fabric, painted red soles, sequins colored a dark red to match, shaped leather bows, and three kinds of beads and rhinestones.

For a long time, the Ruby Slippers were forgotten, along with many other artifacts and papers from the film. When the first pair was discovered in 1970, it became the most sought-after item of MGM memorabilia, selling at auction for $15,000, a huge sum at the time. Subsequent pairs fared even better. In 1988 a pair sold for $150,000, and in 2000 another sold for $660,000. In 2012 Leonardo DiCaprio led a group of donors in buying a pair for the Academy of Motion Picture Arts and Sciences for an undisclosed sum. A pair on loan to the Judy Garland Museum in Grand Rapids, Minnesota, was stolen in 2005, after an exit door window and plexiglass case were broken, but it was recovered by an FBI sting operation in 2018.

That same year, a pair of Ruby Slippers—after

undergoing extensive research and conservation by a team of experts—returned to a display case in a newly renovated wing at the National Museum of American History in Washington, D.C. They are among the most asked-about items at the museum, just one more indication of the prominent place *The Wizard of Oz* still claims in our hearts and minds.

Bibliography

Auxier, Randall E., and Phillip S. Seng, eds. *The Wizard of Oz and Philosophy: Wicked Wisdom of the West.* Chicago: Open Court, 2008.

Campbell, Joseph. *The Hero with a Thousand Faces.* Novato, CA: New World Library, 2008.

Durand, Kevin K., and Mary K. Leigh, eds. *The Universe of Oz: Essays on Baum's Series and Its Progeny.* Jefferson, NC: MacFarland & Co, 2010.

Epstein, Mark. *Thoughts Without a Thinker.* New York: Basic Books, 1995.

Green, Joey. *The Zen of Oz: Ten Spiritual Lessons from Over the Rainbow.* Los Angeles: Renaissance Books, 1998.

Hanh, Thich Nhat. *You Are Here: Discovering the Magic of the Present Moment.* Boston and London: Shambhala

Publications, 2010. Translated from the French by Sherab Chödzin Kohn. Edited by Melvin McLeod.

Harmetz, Aljean. *The Making of the Wizard of Oz*. New York: Alfred A. Knopf, 1977.

Hearn, Michael Patrick. *The Annotated Wizard of Oz: The Wonderful Wizard of Oz by L. Frank Baum; pictures by W. W. Denslow*; with an introduction, notes, and bibliography by Michael Patrick Hearn; preface by Martin Gardner. New York: W. W. Norton & Company, 2000.

Langley, Noel, Florence Ryerson, and Edgar Allan Woolf. *The Wizard of Oz: The Screenplay, Based on the Book by L. Frank Baum*. Edited and with an introduction by Michael Patrick Hearn. New York: Delta Books, 1989.

Loncraine, Rebecca. *The Real Wizard of Oz: The Life and Times of L. Frank Baum*. New York: Gotham Books, 2009.

Rahn, Suzanne. *The Wizard of Oz: Shaping an Imaginary World*. New York: Twayne Publishers; London: Prentice Hall, International, 1998.

Rushdie, Salman. *The Wizard of Oz*. London: British Film Institute, 1992.

Scarfone, Jay, and William Stillman. *The Wizard of Oz: The Official 75th Anniversary Companion*. New York: HarperCollins, 2013.

Acknowledgments

PROFUSE THANKS TO my intrepid publishing team at HarperCollins: Jonathan Burnham, whose enthusiasm set things in motion; Karen Rinaldi, who embodies the insight that editing is an act of love; Hannah Robinson, whose enthusiasm, diligence, and keen observations made this a much better book; Brian Perrin, Laura Cole, Falon Kirby, Bonni Leon-Berman, Nathaniel Knaebel, Shelly Perron, the sales team, and all the many people who worked behind the scenes to put these pages in your hands.

Thank you Andrea Griffith Cash for your tireless efforts to get out the word about this book—and for being one of the very first to try the nine Emeralds on for size.

Anne Edelstein, peerless agent, provided safe harbor in stormy weather and fair. Thank you for your belief in me, for your sage counsel, and for reading all those drafts!

I have been blessed with a family of friends who have accompanied me on my journey down this Yellow Brick Road. Rich Pinto, whose mountain getaway, generosity, and lifelong friendship provide sanctuary, succor, and inspiration. Yehuda Gourvitch, consigliere and friend, whose talent for keeping an eye on the prize kept me from wandering irretrievably far afield. Steve Heidemann, whose generosity as a reader of various drafts has been a priceless gift. Gerry Hull, with thanks for the company, the advice, the prayer hotline, and the hot licks on guitar. Gloria Wilens, Michael Weissman, Mitchell Fink, and Robert Gibralter, whose belief in this book became contagious just when I needed it most. The Washington, D.C., crew—David Vladeck, Mary Pendergast, Bob Young, and Gerry Spann—for your unflagging enthusiasm and steady stream of creative ideas. Mary and Sal, for your hospitality at Plum Cottage, and for access to that amazing vinyl collection. Leigh Anne Couch, for your keen eye and your poet's ear.

Buckets of gratitude to the New Year's Eve crowd at Emerald Isle, with a special shout-out to the Goll-Youngs.

Heartfelt thanks to the true wizards in my life: Scott

Bryce, whose therapeutic insights extend effortlessly into the realm of Oz; Noriko Brantley, who works her magic every week to help keep body and soul together; and Patricia Bradshaw, the family whisperer.

My parents, Walter and Anne Guzzardi, would have taken great pleasure in the publication of this book. My children—Sam, William, and Miriam—have lifted me up from the moment they came into this world and continue to nourish me with their brains, heart, and courage. And, of course, my endlessly patient and loving wife, Isabel Geffner, who has been hearing the words "once I get this book finished . . ." for five years without complaint. You're my Dorothy, Is.

Lastly, I am grateful to all the authors I've had the privilege to work with over the years. Only now that I've written my own book can I truly appreciate the sacred trust you placed in me. I hope I have proved worthy of it.

About the Author

PETER GUZZARDI has worked in publishing for more than forty years. Prominent books he has edited include Stephen Hawking's *A Brief History of Time*, Deepak Chopra's *Ageless Body, Timeless Mind*, Queen Noor's *Leap of Faith*, Susan Cain's *Quiet*, and Douglas Adams's *Mostly Harmless*. An independent editor and writer, he lives in Chapel Hill, North Carolina.

He can be reached at www.peterguzzardi.com.